Understanding Democratic Curriculum Leadership

D1125037

99

Understanding Democratic Curriculum Leadership

EDITED BY

James G. Henderson and Kathleen R. Kesson

FOREWORD BY **William F. Pinar**

Teachers College, Columbia University
New York and London

Published by Teachers College Press, 1234 Amsterdam Avenue, New York, NY 10027

Copyright © 1999 by Teachers College, Columbia University

All rights reserved. No part of this publication may be reproduced or transmitted in any form or by any means, electronic or mechanical, including photocopy, or any information storage and retrieval system, without permission from the publisher.

Library of Congress Cataloging-in-Publication Data

Understanding democratic curriculum leadership / edited by James G. Henderson and Kathleen R. Kesson ; foreword by William F. Pinar.
    p.   cm.
   Includes bibliographical references and index.
   ISBN 0-8077-3827-1 (cloth : alk. paper). — ISBN 0-8077-3826-3 (pbk. : alk. paper)
   1. Curriculum planning—United States.   2. Liberty.   3. Educational leadership—United States.   I. Henderson, James George. II. Kesson, Kathleen R.
LB2806.15.U53   1999
375'.001'0973—dc21   98-50770

ISBN 0-8077-3826-3 (paper)
ISBN 0-8077-3827-1 (cloth)

Printed on acid-free paper
Manufactured in the United States of America

06 05 04 03 02 01 00 99   8 7 6 5 4 3 2 1

Contents

Foreword

Interest in knowledge for the sake of knowledge, in thinking for the sake
of the free play of thought, is necessary then to emancipation of practical
life—to make it rich and progressive.
                                                    —John Dewey, *How We Think*

Understanding has to do with relationships.
                                                    —Boyd Henry Bode, *How We Learn*

AMERICAN EFFORTS TO UNDERSTAND the inextricable relationship between
democracy and education received their quintessential expression in
John Dewey's (1916) canonical work on the subject. Nearly a century
later we are still straining to teach our constituents, and ourselves, this
simultaneously simple but complicated and profound fact. In our time,
the effort has been complicated by what Joe Kincheloe (Chapter 5, this
volume) characterizes as the "crisis of democracy." Certainly the sense of
powerlessness and political alienation that, for instance, African
Americans and many others have experienced since the nation's birth
seems now extended to many heterosexual White men, the nation's historical, prototypical civic subject. Now the straight White man of property
also feels adrift in a dead sea of political stasis.

While current conditions require of us educators greater determi-
nation, our pedagogical imperative to teach—and to perform in Judith
Butler's (1993) not self-evident sense—democratization remains. While
"praxis" has undergone the same conceptual degradation many popularized concepts suffer—from meaning something definite to meaning
something vague and now meaning not much at all—it was once a conceptual rallying point for our generation's commitment to democracy and
education. Theory and practice, we were sure, would become dialectically
interrelated, leading us and our students to higher levels, in Freire's
(1968) term, in a process of conscientization. There was a certain genera-
tional solidarity in that belief, suggested in James Henderson's remark
(Chapter 7, this volume) that he has come to view "the American story

as inspiring and frustratingly unfulfilled." That is an apt and succinct expression of how many of us feel. Somehow the two—inspiration and frustration—keep him, keep us, moving on, still, despite the odds, despite the reality, committed to democracy and education.

James G. Henderson and Kathleen R. Kesson are clearly so committed. This commitment is everywhere evident in this book, "designed," as Henderson writes, "to support a deepening critical understanding of *democratic* curriculum leadership." Henderson quotes John Dewey to remind us that democracy is not just pulling levers on a voting machine, that it "is a way of life. We have yet to realize it is a way of personal life and one which provides a moral standard for personal conduct." It is, of course, tied to freedom. Maxine Greene (1988), Henderson notes, "presents a complex, layered understanding of *human freedom.*" He finds in Nel Noddings' (1984) work one of the book's key ideas, that of a caring learning community, what he calls a "forest" idea, as in not being able to see the forest for the trees. "Maintaining this balance between 'forest' and 'trees' is not possible," Henderson explains, "without establishing a rhythm between attention to the details of curricular change and continuing *critical reflection* on the 'big picture' of this reform effort." To "perform" this rhythm, Henderson and Kesson have selected four critical topics from the tradition of curriculum studies, to be discussed by prominent curriculum scholars: (1) curriculum deliberation by Gail McCutcheon, (2) reflexive systems by Noel Gough, (3) cultural criticism by Joe Kincheloe, and (4) educational mythopoetics by Kathleen Kesson. There is as well a reflection by a public school teacher named Kerrin McCadden.

It is quite clear that Henderson and Kesson appreciate the complexity of the current situation in the schools. They understand that democratic curriculum reform cannot proceed simply, as on a flowchart, as if procedural consensus could resolve political conflict. In the past, but especially now, curriculum is the site of political, racial, gendered, and theological dispute. The present situation is very much contested; the curriculum has been claimed by many and often opposed constituencies. As Henderson remarks (with understatement), "in most settings, such dramatic reform is not possible without a carefully cultivated dialogue among all *curriculum stakeholders:* educational administrators, teachers, teacher aides, students, students' parents, school psychologists, social workers, community, business, and religious leaders, and so on." It is a very crowded overheated room indeed, and one that calls one to cultivate, if one aspires to provide "curriculum leadership," among other things, the art of deliberation.

Joseph Schwab (1978) must be credited with emphasizing the significance of this art, an art associated with disciplined conversation. It

surfaces again as a major theme in this collection. Understand that "deliberation" is no detached, abstract exchange among Schwab and his University of Chicago colleagues. (Gail McCutcheon points out that her view
of "deliberation" is less "formal" than Schwab's.) Given the complex and
often contentious character of curriculum, deliberation is now closer to a
form of curriculum politics, as Gail acknowledges: "Conflict is the engine
driving deliberations, and alternatives are the fuel." However, the process
is not exclusively political; it is also moral. McCutcheon informs us: "Deliberation has a moral nature in that it is not a totally objective, value-
free enterprise, nor should it be. . . . In addition, deliberation is a social
enterprise because the concept of the 'good' democratic society informs
collaborative decisions and thus provides an ethical context for all decisions." By depicting deliberation as collaborative and democratic, McCutcheon's model of curriculum leadership echoes certain feminist models of
consciousness raising. Her sense of deliberation has little in common with
hierarchical, patriarchal, or "top-down" models of curriculum implementation.

How does "deliberation" as a key element in curriculum leadership
function in the school as a social system? Noel Gough helps us think
about that question, suggesting it might be useful "to think of a system as
some kind of organism." But it is not just *any* organism, is it? Noel thinks
of the system as a "wild animal" that needs to be "tamed" before it can
be made to "do some good." Perhaps the organism Gough has in the back
of his mind is the macho male, the somewhat but not entirely mythical
coach-promoted-to-principal? Yes, that's a stereotype, but the majority of
school administrators *are* male, and while we don't tend to think of them
as "wild men," perhaps they do, even so, require a little taming. Otherwise they can tend to think the bureaucratic system is, well, theirs. Procedures—strategies of convenience and efficiency—sometimes become sac-
rosanct, as if they were a set of commandments, rather than (as Gough
suggests, borrowing Gibson's description of cyberspace) the "consensual
hallucination" that the bureaucracy in fact is.

It is narrative theory or curriculum understood as storytelling, Gough
argues, that "provides us with many critical and creative conceptual tools
for both understanding and improving the practice of curriculum leadership." He quotes Madeleine Grumet's famous definition of curriculum
as the "collective story we tell our children about our past, our present,
and our future." Not that this is a finished or unchanging story—Grumet
(1988) employs hermeneutics, autobiography, and feminist theory to
show that—but a social experience, much more, well, I would say con-
versational (Pinar, Reynolds, Slattery, & Taubman, 1995, p. 848), McCutcheon would say deliberative, and Bill Doll (1993)—whom Noel credits

with making "perhaps . . . the most practical contribution to curriculum leadership"—might say chaotic, if in a different sense than the vernacular. Certainly the point would be not to turn curriculum documents into monuments, as Foucault warned in a different context and Gough nicely reiterates.

From another tradition—critical theory—Joe Kincheloe thinks about the problem of curriculum in terms of the present social and political crisis. "The last quarter of the twentieth century," he tells us, "has been marked by a crisis of democracy—a crisis seldom referenced in the public conversation or in educational institutions." Joe argues for a kind of "critical democracy" that would be characterized by a hermeneutical practice. I think Joe would agree with me that this crisis is also a gendered one, and that much of the reactionary political response of the past 30 years can be understood as (although not reduced to) an effort to reassert white heterosexual male privilege. Mad men don't tend to engage in dialogue; they make accusations, often quote scripture, all the while demanding that things be set right.

Kathleen Kesson wants things set right too, but she appreciates that both ends and means are not self-evident, but must be decided together, democratically. To reflect on these complicated issues, Kathleen turns to mythopoetics, which points to "the profoundly personal lived experience of human beings, in all of its depth and complexity." This idea—James Macdonald (1995) was the pioneer here—includes, Kathleen notes, "autobiography and personal narrative." "Stories are so pervasive throughout the world and throughout history," she continues, "that one might assume, as does curriculum theorist Kieran Egan (1986), that our brains are somehow 'hard-wired' to respond to the narrative form." "In Vermont," Kesson reports, "personal development is one of the primary categories for curriculum development. . . . the inclusion of the self in the curriculum . . . [is] mostly evident in aspects of whole language programs such as journal writing and reader response logs." She points out that "autobiographical work sometimes has been misunderstood as 'asocial,' but scholars, such as Janet Miller (1990), emphasize the collaborative and social character of such research." Kathleen summarizes well: "The work of curriculum leaders occurs in complex political networks, which are underpinned by multiple subjectivities, disparate beliefs, and complex webs of meanings. People's visions of what schooling should be are intimately connected with their visions of what constitutes the good life, the viable society. These meanings and beliefs sometimes lie below the surface of consciousness, and it falls to educational leaders to make the tacit, taken-for-granted realities explicit, problematic. It is an uneasy position to be in" (Chapter 6, this volume).

In the concluding chapter of the book, Henderson, Kesson, and Kerrin McCadden reflect on what has transpired herein, namely, an effort to elaborate "the meaning of a *caring learning community*." The curriculum of such a community integrates "critical conversation with progressive practice." This means a democratic inclusion of all involved in the educational project, most particularly the practitioner. "By concluding with a practitioner's voice," they write, "we are emphasizing the point that the day-to-day, politically demanding and stressful work of democratic curriculum reform takes place in public schools, not in the minds of curriculum theorists."

Deliberation—both solo and group, as Gail McCutcheon points out—involves storytelling, what Freire (1968) termed "dialogical encounter." Of course, this order of conversation is not easily conducted in today's schools. Why? "The potential dynamism of the curriculum deliberation process has been constrained," Kathleen Kesson observes, ". . . because the discourses of accountability, standards, and best practices came to overshadow the discourses of justice, equity, caring, and human development." What to do? "I believe," Kathleen writes, "that we must engage in moral conversations and in acts of political solidarity with our colleagues in the field who struggle daily to actualize emancipatory ideals." And this is, it seems to me, what this book does.

That success is evident in the practitioner's piece. A teacher of English in a small city in rural New England, Kerrin McCadden understands the gendered character of the theory/practice relationship. "Like any self-respecting Victorian era woman," she muses, "classroom teachers have been given too much lace to tat and too many knick-knacks to dust to nurture ideas." The pressure she describes is a classic instance of "hyperrationalization" (Pinar et al., 1995, p. 667), an abstraction that McCadden's description renders tellingly concrete. She is clear that gendered insistence on "productivity" puts an end to curriculum as an authentic and complicated conversation. A different set of images and ideas—McCadden settles nicely on "generative"—is required if we are, thinking of Noel Gough's comment, to hallucinate a different social reality. A sense of the "generative," she writes, "threads its way through almost every idea in this book. Even when we are being reminded to deconstruct, it is for the sake of continued change and growth." I agree.

Change and growth are good things, as feminists have shown, that is, if they are self-directed. Change and growth become euphemisms for compliance when they are directed by others. Those 1970s women's consciousness-raising groups, for instance, rarely were led by men; after all, it was women who labored to find voice, express silenced realities, and discover the solidarity that inheres in the experience of oppression. Freire spoke about "generative themes" emerging from the authentic dialogue of the oppressed. Articulating these themes not only heightens the awareness of those who are, in Freire's language, submerged in reality, but they enable the participants to understand the provisionality of that reality, how it might be acted upon, transformed. Characterized by deliberation and storytelling, democratic curriculum leadership, is, among other things, such a generative practice. Perhaps we can understand continuing resistance to it—from within the field as well as from outside—if we keep in mind that it is also a gendered practice.

Recall that, despite the large number of men in the profession, the figure of the schoolteacher, in the American imagination, is female. Especially since the rise of the public school in the nineteenth century, it is women who have tended to go into teaching, especially at the elementary level. That the figure of the American schoolteacher is female is key to unraveling persisting confusions regarding and resistances to the democratization of the theory/practice relationship. This is illustrated by two responses to the observation, made by Pinar and colleagues (1995) in *Understanding Curriculum*, that a paradigmatic shift has occurred in curriculum studies over the past 30 years. This shift, which Henderson and Kesson mention, was from "curriculum development" toward "understanding curriculum." What does that mean?

In abbreviated form, here are the facts: Schools are no longer under the jurisdiction (which was always more professional and political than legal) of education professors. Multiple "stakeholders" (not the least among them the textbook publishers) have created something that tries to look like curriculum consensus but is in fact "gridlock," so that genuine (not just rhetorical) reforms—let alone revolutions—in practice are unlikely, and certainly unlikely to be led by university-based curriculum scholars and researchers. This is not to say that we in the university have, for instance, lost interest in teachers or in schooling, or that we have been seduced by subjects more interesting and exciting (although some students of cultural studies might say that). The simple, if for some unassimilable, truth is that our influence has decreased over the past 30 years, not only due to a more complicated and contentious political and cultural terrain in which curricular issues are now situated, but also due to a certain devaluation of education professors generally. This devaluation followed not only attacks from the arts and sciences professors in the 1950s (Arthur Bestor [1953] was the most visible, I suppose) and continuing to the present time, for instance, Adler (1982), Bloom (1987), and Hirsch (1987), but more important, the Kennedy administration's curriculum reform movement in the 1960s, the leaders of which were discipline-based practitioners in the university (such as physicists), not curriculum developers in schools of education. These two developments—an increasingly complex and multiply influenced school situation (from the right wing, etc.) and a devaluation in the political stock of education and (specifically) curriculum professors—plus a third and sometimes related development—a movement toward "theory" and scholarly understanding rather than bureaucratic proceduralism (imprinted in the famous Tyler Rationale [Tyler, 1949])—resulted in a reconceptualized field of curriculum studies.

Because traditional curriculum development was no longer an option for curriculum generalists by the 1970s, and not wanting to be left looking for something to do (as Schwab entitled his 1983 essay), we formulated ways for the traditional concerns of the field—such as asking the fundamental curriculum question, What knowledge is of most worth?—to be re-expressed, this time via teachers' interpretations of the textbooks chosen by others. Interpretation involves, as this volume indicates, deliberation and storytelling, all laced with politics, race, and gender. Phenomenology (including hermeneutics) as well as poststructuralism, autobiography and biography, aesthetics, theology, international developments, and strictly institutional concerns thematize contemporary scholarly efforts to understand curriculum. Now we understand that curriculum is not only school and district guidelines, textbooks, and objectives, but that "complicated conversation" in which teachers and students engage each other as well as the textbook material in, as this book succinctly puts it, a caring learning community.

The responses to these observations have been peculiar and revealing. They underline, I believe, the gendered character of the theory/practice relationship. If we are to understand the inextricable relations between democracy and education, we are obligated, it turns out, to challenge patriarchy. For if the figure of the American schoolteacher is female, the figure of the American college professor is male. For "theory" (associated with the university) to acknowledge that "practice" (associated with the school) is no longer able or willing to accept/follow its dictates and advice, amounts to acknowledging that women no longer are dependent on or require men. Nothing works better than an acknowledgment like that to persuade some straight White men that it's time to quote scripture. And in one form or another, that is precisely what critics have done.

One kind of response to the history of the field reported in *Understanding Curriculum* has been reminiscent of those (often) southern preachers who resort to quoting the Old Testament to support their (usually "his") idea of "tradition." One critic actually quoted from the 1862 Morrill Act that established new agricultural and mechancial colleges with explicit vocational missions. This is an odd version of a sacred text, wouldn't you say, but it was cited as if it were: to show the errors of the contemporary field. So it was written, so it shall be: We in the university must never abandon our charge to inform "practice." A second kind of response has been, well let's say, more New Testament, in which the reviewers concluded their essay by "witnessing." They recounted how they had traveled among the multitudes (i.e., schoolteachers) with timeless curriculum ideas, thereby raising them up from, well if not the dead, maybe routine, two fates not so very different when all is said and done.

What provoked the preaching, some of it in the category of "old time religion" and some of it a more New Testament–style tale of salvation? Why would critics misread this reporting of the facts as a kind of theory deserting practice, or as a heretical distortion of tradition? If we keep in mind that the figure of the American schoolteacher is female and that the figure of the American college professor is male, the puzzle becomes clarified. One current of it is, I suppose, a sense of male loyalty to the female, not wanting to leave her in the lurch, wanting to be helpful. A few male curriculum scholars' wives are in fact schoolteachers; to speak of theory and practice parting company must feel to them a little like, if not a divorce, at least a separation. But another current—and here is the locus of the anger, the preaching—is a reassertion of heterosexual male privilege. It is our job—as professionals, that is, "men"—to tell teachers, that is, women, what to do; theory must guide practice. Of course, more than a few practitioners ask us to tell them what to do, although I think that is often an expression of resistance to the privileged and gendered site of theory, pointing out as it sometimes does that we experts do not know how to change schools.

To suggest that we men have lost our historical position of privilege and influence with schools, that now both scholars *and* practitioners must reflect *together* on education—in theoretically informed ways—as something of "equals," implies an equality of partnership between men and women that is yet to be realized in American society at large, and certainly not in curriculum studies. Some injured men—ah, a crisis of democracy, is it?—resort to the Old Testament, citing nineteenth-century legislation that, presumably, consecrates our position as head of the (school)household. Others inspire crestfallen readers with tales of preaching to masses, converting them, by the power of the word, to new life. Behind both reactionary responses lies a reassertion of traditional gender roles and in particular the privileged location of the heterosexual White male, as these are encoded professionally and intellectually in the theory/practice relationship.

So "understanding democratic curriculum leadership" runs up against not just right-wing crazies, but our close colleagues who are not eager to abandon what seems to them ordained, if not by nature, if not by God, then at least by the Morrill Act. I applaud Jim Henderson and Kathleen Kesson for fighting the good fight, for insisting on democratization despite these profoundly antidemocratic currents. "Deliberation" and "storytelling" as elucidated here are nearly unknown arts, in the university as well as in the school. Democratization is a gendered as well as political and pedagogical aspiration. When we deliberate and tell stories, let us speak of a day when traditional and unjust divisions of labor are memories only, when men regard women not as practice to be guided, but as equal and respected colleagues engaged in that complicated conversation with our children that is the curriculum.

—William F. Pinar

REFERENCES

Adler, M. (1982). *The Paideia proposal.* New York: Macmillan.

Bloom, A. (1987). *The closing of the American mind.* New York: Simon & Schuster.

Bestor, A. (1953). *Educational wastelands: The retreat from learning in our public schools.* Urbana: University of Illinois Press.

Bode, B. H. (1940). *How we learn.* Boston: Heath.

Butler, J. (1993). *Bodies that matter: On the discursive limits of "sex."* New York & London: Routledge.

Dewey, J. (1910). *How we think.* Boston: Heath.

Dewey, J. (1916). *Democracy and education.* New York: Macmillan.

Doll, W. E., Jr. (1993). *A post-modern perspective on curriculum.* New York: Teachers College Press.

Egan, K. (1990). *Romantic understanding: The development of rationality and imagination, ages 8–15.* New York & London: Routledge.

Egan, K. (1992). *Imagination in teaching and learning.* Chicago: University of Chicago Press.

Freire, P. (1968). *Pedagogy of the oppressed.* New York: Seabury.

Greene, M. (1988). *The dialectic of freedom.* New York: Teachers College Press.

Grumet, M. R. (1988). *Bitter milk: Women and teaching.* Amherst: University of Massachusetts Press.

Hirsch, E. D. (1987). *Cultural literacy: What every American needs to know.* Boston: Houghton Mifflin.

Macdonald, B. J. (Ed.). (1995). *Theory as a prayerful act: The collected essays of James B. Macdonald.* New York: Peter Lang.

Miller, J. L. (1990). *Creating spaces and finding voices: Teachers collaborating for empowerment.* Albany: State University of New York Press.

Noddings, N. (1984). *Caring.* Berkeley: University of California Press.

Pinar, W. F., Reynolds, W. M., Slattery, P., & Taubman, P. M. (1995). *Understanding curriculum: An introduction to the study of historical and contemporary curriculum discourses.* New York: Peter Lang.

Schwab, J. (1978). *Science, curriculum and liberal education: Selected essays* (I. Westbury & N. D. Wilkof, Eds.). Chicago: University of Chicago Press.

Schwab, J. (1983, Fall). The practical 4: Something for curriculum professors to do. *Curriculum Inquiry, 13,* 239–266.

Tyler, R. W. (1949). *Basic principles of curriculum and instruction.* Chicago: University of Chicago Press.

Preface

THE STUDY OF CURRICULUM has become more varied, more intellectually complicated, and more vital than ever before. The field only recently has been emerging from something of a "paradigm war," begun almost 20 years ago, during which scholars who were committed to liberation from stifling curriculum traditions introduced a number of new themes and sources into their work. The field has now, as we note in Chapter 1, been "reconceptualized" rather successfully, and theories of curriculum, drawing on European philosophical discourses as well as current developments in feminist theory, psychoanalysis, social theory, and phenomenology (to name just a few of the many influences), have become immeasurably more sophisticated. One unfortunate outcome of this otherwise fruitful development has been the distancing of curriculum theory from the actual work that goes on in schools. Despite the efforts of some theorists to remain connected to the realm of schools, the current situation, for the most part, represents a continuing theory/practice split.

The tension between "theory" and "practice" is an historical tension. Defined by Aristotle as distinct categories of knowledge, *theoria* (theoretical knowledge) and *praxis* (practical knowledge) came to represent a division that remained conceptually viable through the historical period of medieval scholasticism. Following that period, throughout what we have come to call the Enlightenment, philosophical debates continued to take shape around this historical dualism, and philosophers such as Kant and Hegel modified and extended traditional concepts. It is perhaps a testimony to the complexity of the debates that controversies exist today over distinctions between, as well as the nature of the relationship between, theoretical and practical knowledge. Nowhere is this debate more lively than in the field of curriculum.

Few curriculum theorists would deny that their theorizing is itself a type of "practice." And few people engaged in school-based practices of curriculum (teachers, curriculum developers and designers, policy makers, and administrators) would acknowledge that their practice is uninformed by theory. Theorists and practitioners, however, may disagree on the constitutive nature of "theory" (Whose knowledge? How was it constructed? Whose interests are served by it?) as well as the direction of the relationship (Should theory precede action? Does theory evolve out of action? Or is there a seamless sort of theory-in-action that overrides questions of directionality?). Theorists and practitioners reside in differing language communities. The work of curriculum theorists takes place largely in university settings, in which reading, research, writing, theorizing, and publication are valued and supported (although many professors would argue that support for these aspects of their work is inadequate!). It is in the vested interest of theorists to develop ever more sophisticated language schemes to present increasingly complex ideas. School-based curriculum workers, on the other hand, are busy with children, colleagues, school boards, administrators, lesson planning, parents, and innumerable bureaucratic expectations in their day-to-day work in schools. As teacher Kerrin McCadden points out in the concluding chapter, the very structure of teachers' work precludes the kind of intellectual and conceptual engagement taken for granted by curriculum theorists. If we are, however, to move into a "Second Wave" of curriculum theorizing, a movement that might link the major ideas that constitute the contemporary field of study to colleagues in the elementary and secondary schools (Pinar, 1988), then we must develop language, structures, and processes that might facilitate the necessary conversations about theory, practice, and the relationships between them. This book is premised on our underlying commitment to this movement.

The reconceptualized curriculum field takes as its fundamentals a deep commitment to human development as well as a commitment to the increasing democratization of the public sphere. These interdependent commitments—to self-actualization and to social liberation—have largely superseded older, technical commitments to learning theory, the structures of knowledge and the disciplines, and curriculum design and development. These current commitments of the field explain the recent engagement with discourses of gender, race, sexuality, psychoanalysis, politics, and culture, as curriculum theorists have sought to unravel the mysterious ways that schools, in spite of the rhetoric of "equal opportunity," tend to reproduce the inequalities of previous generations, and tend not to be places where all students make rich and lasting meaning for themselves. Curriculum leaders (and we include here teachers involved in curriculum redesign and textbook adoption, curriculum coordinators, staff development specialists, and administrators who take an active interest in curriculum matters) who share these fundamental commitments to democracy and human development are overwhelmed with many other expectations: that all students will live up to high "standards," that test scores will be high, that assessments will provide the accountability that communities are looking for, that schools will be drug and violence free, and that the learning needs of all children will be met. And this is just the short list! In the face of the myriad demands on curriculum leaders, it is not surprising that they have paid scant attention to the reconceptualized curriculum field with its diverse and sophisticated set of critical projects, and that the field has failed to have a significant impact on curriculum work in schools.

It is our premise that the work of theorists and the work of practitioners will be mutually enriched by engagement in what we are calling the "hermeneutic circle," that is, the continuous reflection on the details of practice in light of selected critical theorizing, and, reciprocally, the continuous critique of critical theorizing in light of practical experience. It is in this spirit that we have designed this book to support the continuing professional development of curriculum leaders who wish to carry on the moral conversation about democracy and human development. While the book is in part an effort to heal the wounds of the theory/practice split in the field, the authors acknowledge their own perpetuation of this split with their occasional use of such dichotomous terms as "theoretician" and "practitioner" as analytical categories. As in the analysis of other dualisms (body/mind, nature/culture), we suffer from a lack of language that might illuminate new relationships and new categories. We have tried to foreground this tension, both in the developmental process of the book project and in the writing of it.

As you will read in Chapter 1, the book was constructed around a series of conversations, in which a group of Vermont curriculum leaders read and critiqued four curriculum theory essays, and provided valuable feedback to the authors about ways that their ideas could be made more accessible and more relevant. While the other three chapter authors had access to the "hermeneutic circle" only via videotape, I was privileged to enjoy the rich face-to-face conversations generated by these topics. I would like to thank all of the members of this group, who are introduced individually in Chapter 2, for helping me to refine my thinking and better articulate my ideas. I think that my chapter on "mythopoetics" was improved greatly by their insightful critique and suggestions. A special thanks goes to Kerrin McCadden for her work on the concluding chapter of the book. I believe that she captures the very real dilemmas facing teachers who seek to be the intellectually engaged, democratically committed practitioners that our schools so desperately need. My appreciation for the work that teachers do and the struggles they face daily deepened as we all worked together on this project.

A number of other acknowledgments are in order. The opportunity for Jim, Kerrin, and me to work on this project together was supported by the John Dewey Project on Progressive Education at the College of Education and Social Services at the University of Vermont, and we are grateful for that support. Thanks as well to Ron Miller and the Bellwether School for making space available for our study group meetings. While the sound of children's voices occasionally drowned out short sections of the videotape when school let out for the day, at those times we were happily reminded of our purposes for engaging in the critical study of curriculum. Thanks as well to Gay Fawcett for her thorough and insightful reading of the finished manuscript.

We had the opportunity to share our work-in-progress in a number of venues throughout the writing of the book, including the JCT (Journal of Curriculum Theorizing) Conference, the annual meetings of the American Educational Research Association, and the Professors of Curriculum meeting. Our colleagues provided us with many critical insights that contributed to the final product. And finally, our thanks to Brian Ellerbeck, at Teachers College Press, for his support, encouragement, and editorial suggestions from the conception of this project through to its finish. We hope that this book captures the rich, multiperspective feel of the contemporary field of curriculum, and that it invites those who consider themselves democratic curriculum leaders, whether they work in schools or universities, state departments or central offices, to partake of this ongoing conversation.

—Kathleen R. Kesson

REFERENCE

Pinar, W. F. (1988). *Contemporary curriculum discourses*. Scottsdale, AZ: Gorsuch Scarisbrick.

The Journey of Democratic Curriculum Leadership: An Overview

JAMES G. HENDERSON

THIS BOOK HAS BEEN DESIGNED to support a deepening critical understanding of *democratic* curriculum leadership. This first chapter will provide an overview of how the book has been organized to meet this goal. We begin with an examination of the more familiar "managerial" interpretation of curriculum leadership and then turn to the philosophy, ethics, and activities of democratic curriculum leadership as understood through the work of John Dewey and, particularly, Maxine Greene. This contrast establishes the critical frame of reference for this text. Four critical curriculum study topics that provide important insight into the practice of democratic curriculum leadership will then be introduced. It is the premise of this book that curriculum practitioners who are interested in a Deweyan understanding of *democratic* curriculum leadership will find the study of these four topics to be beneficial to their work.

CURRICULUM LEADERSHIP AS MANAGERIAL CONTROL

Most educational practitioners have some exposure to curriculum leadership. Perhaps they have served on a textbook adoption committee; or perhaps they have been asked to review and redesign an educational program. They may have developed guiding materials for a new course or teaching unit; and they may have made presentations to, or even been a

Understanding Democratic Curriculum Leadership. Copyright © 1999 by Teachers College, Columbia University. All rights reserved. ISBN 0-8077-3826-3 (pbk), ISBN 0-8077-3827-1 (cloth). Prior to photocopying items for classroom use, please contact the Copyright Clearance Center, Customer Service, 222 Rosewood Dr., Danvers, MA 01923, USA, tel. (508) 750-8400.

member of, a school board. Whatever their curricular experiences—as a teacher, administrator, school counselor, parent, community leader, or other educational stakeholder—the odds are that their curriculum work occurred in a context of *managerial control*. Their activities were guided by a set of predetermined outcome statements (behavioral objectives, pupil performance objectives, instructional goals, and so on) and/or by standardized assessment instruments (norm-referenced tests, state proficiency examinations, uniform student portfolios, and so on). In other words, they were told by others (people referred to as educational "policy makers," "managers," "administrators," or "leaders") how to orient their curriculum practices.

As Maxcy (1991) notes, the concern with the *managerial control* of educational activity, which has its roots in the emergence of nineteenth-century bureaucratic organizations in many sectors of society, occurred "against a backdrop of business-related philosophies that called for a shift away from humanistic and personal values to the good of the company" (p. 2). Sergiovanni (1992) characterizes this control orientation as the "managerial mystique," which he summarizes as follows:

> In practice, the managerial mystique represents a tacit compact among too many policymakers, administrators, and academics, which places process before substance and form before function. So strongly does the mystique adhere to belief in the right methods that the methods themselves become surrogates for results: It also holds so firmly to the belief in management controls, as the way to overcome human shortcomings and enhance productivity, that the controls become ends in themselves.
>
> The result is an emphasis on doing things right, at the expense of doing the right things. In schools, improvement plans become substitutes for improvement outcomes. Scores on teacher-appraisal systems become substitutes for good teaching. Accumulation of credits in courses and in service workshops becomes a substitute for changes in practice. Discipline plans become substitutes for student control. Leadership styles become substitutes for purpose and substance. Congeniality becomes a substitute for collegiality. Cooperation becomes a substitute for commitment. Compliance becomes a substitute for results. Where the managerial mystique rules, school administrators are forced to do rather than decide, to implement rather than lead. (p. 4)

Sergiovanni (1992) observes that the preoccupation with managerial control often leads to the emergence of two major problems in modern organizational life: *trained incapacity* and *goal displacement*. Trained incapacity refers to the "tendency to focus knowledge, attention, and skills so narrowly that principals and teachers become incapable of thinking and acting beyond their prescribed roles" (Sergiovanni, 1992, p. 5); while goal displacement is "the tendency for schools to lose sight of their purposes, allowing instrumental processes and procedures to become ends in themselves" (p. 5).

Early curriculum study projects in the United States generally encouraged this managerial control of educational practice. Curriculum studies is a "subdivision" of education (Schubert, 1986). Historically, scholarly projects in this subdivision have focused on "the relationships among the school subjects as well as issues within the individual school subjects themselves and with the relationships between the curriculum and the world" (Pinar, Reynolds, Slattery, & Taubman, 1995, p. 6). Although there are influential curriculum study documents that can be traced back to, at least, Plato's *The Republic* (trans. 1956), the publication of Franklin Bobbitt's *The Curriculum* in 1918 arguably can be considered the beginning of formal curriculum studies in the United States (Jackson, 1992; Pinar et al., 1995). This book established the precedent that the focus of curriculum studies should be on creating and sustaining institutional curriculum development processes. Pinar and colleagues (1995) describe this focus as the institutional "text" of curriculum studies, which they characterize as follows: "Understanding curriculum as institutionalized text suggests understanding curriculum as it functions bureaucratically . . . ; [it is] an ameliorative approach linked explicitly to the everyday functioning of the institution" (p. 661).

Between 1918 and 1969, institutional curriculum development was a dominant concern of curriculum studies. The Tyler Rationale (Tyler, 1949), which is a refinement of Bobbitt's curriculum development prescriptions (Jackson, 1992), emerged as the major curriculum study document of this period. The Tyler Rationale is designed to promote thoughtful curriculum leadership based on locally relevant interpretations of educational standards. It guides curriculum deliberations over four questions:

- What educational purposes should the school seek to attain?
- How can learning experiences be selected that are likely to be useful in attaining these objectives?
- How can learning experiences be organized for effective instruction?
- How can the effectiveness of learning experiences be evaluated?

Although not necessarily the intent of his pragmatic book, Tyler's curriculum leadership rationale generally was adapted to serve the purpose of *managing* educational practice.[1] Deliberation over "educational purposes" often was interpreted as establishing a testable set of performance objectives. Decisions over relevant "learning experiences" frequently were made by curriculum committees that would adopt standardized textbooks. The organization of the "learning experiences" customarily was interpreted as the establishment of scope and sequence policies, and accountability systems frequently were created to handle the educational evaluations.

Beginning in 1969, curriculum scholars began to establish critical distance from this "managerial" approach to curriculum inquiry. The field of curriculum studies was "reconceptualized" (Pinar, 1975) to focus on a diverse set of critical projects. Because this edited book is a product of this reconceptualist heritage, a brief overview of the history of curriculum studies between 1969 and the present date will be provided later in this chapter—after the practice of *democratic curriculum leadership* has been introduced.

DEMOCRACY AS A MORAL WAY OF LIVING

Democratic curriculum leadership cannot be defined without first clarifying the understanding of "democracy" that is being used to qualify this practice. This step must be taken because "democracy" as a normative term—as a value-based guide to the "good" life—is interpreted in many different ways (Barber, 1984; Beyer, 1996; Snauwaert, 1993). In 1939, on the eve of World War II, the American philosopher, John Dewey (1939/1989), contemplated the challenges that democratic societies faced from the Communist Soviet Union and fascist Germany:

> The democratic road is the hard one to take. It is the road which places the greatest burden of responsibility upon the greatest number of human beings. Backsets and deviations occur and will continue to occur. But that which is its own weakness at particular times is its strength in the long course of human history. Just because the cause of democratic freedom is the cause of the fullest possible realization of human potentialities, the latter when they are suppressed and opposed will in time rebel and demand an opportunity for manifestation. We have advanced far enough to say that democracy is a way of life. We have yet to realize that it is a way of personal life and one which provides a moral standard for personal conduct. (pp. 100–101)

This approach to "democracy" as a *moral way of living* will serve as the normative referent for curriculum leadership in this book. This approach is based on an inquiry-based, growth-oriented understanding that emphasizes the connection between democracy and education (Dewey,

1916). Snauwaert (1993) characterizes this interpretation as a "developmental" understanding of democracy: "From the perspective of this [democratic] tradition, human development rather than efficiency is the ultimate standard upon which systems of governance should be chosen and evaluated" (p. 5).

In a significant philosophical essay entitled *The Dialectic of Freedom*, Maxine Greene (1988) provides a current and insightful discussion of this "developmental" conception of democracy and education. She writes in the spirit of *open-ended inquiry*, not *true belief*—a distinction that lies at the heart of a Deweyan interpretation of democracy. Dewey (1938/1963) describes his democratic faith as an "end in view." An end in view is different from a precise belief. It is an organizing ideal that forever remains open to diverse perspectives. Carlson (1997) characterizes Dewey's democratic end in view as a "fuzzy" utopianism. It is a moral understanding of life that is continually open to re-interpretation or, in Dewey's language, to "reconstruction." A Deweyan democrat does not bring ideological closure to his/her "faith," knowing full well that only through continuing inquiry can this democratic way of life be practiced. Greene (1988) articulates this point of view when she writes:

> I hope to develop a view of education for freedom that will take into account our political and social realities as well as the human condition itself. I hope to communicate a sense of things that is neither contemplative or self-regarding, a mood in which new initiatives can be imagined and dimensions of experience transformed. It is, actually, in the process of effecting transformations that the human self is created and re-created. Dewey, like the existential thinkers, did not believe that the self was ready-made or pre-existent; it was, he said, "something in continuous formation through choice of action" (Dewey, 1916, p. 408). (pp. 21–22)

In a spirit of continually broadening one's "horizons" (Gadamer, 1975), Greene (1988) notes that perspectives on human freedom can never "be finished or complete. There is always more. There is always possibility. And this is where the space opens for the pursuit of freedom" (p. 128).

As she philosophically examines the connections between democracy and education, Greene (1988) presents a complex, layered understanding of *human freedom:* "Freedom cannot be conceived apart from a matrix of social, economic, cultural, and psychological conditions. It is within the matrix that selves take shape or are created through choice of action" (p. 80). She wants the reader to understand that her inquiries are based on an understanding of reality as "interpreted experience" grounded in "sedimented meanings" (p. xii).

Greene (1988) further understands that this layered understanding of human freedom demands a sophisticated deliberative praxis—an "experimental" practice informed by a multidimensional critical awareness. Locating her inquiry project in the context of the best of American progressivist and pragmatic thought, she notes that such individuals as Oliver Wendell Holmes, Thorstein Veblen, Vernon Louis Parrington, William James, John Dewey, Lincoln Steffens, Charles Beard, and Jane Addams all "shared a profound faith in hypothetical and empirical inquiries; and they shared an understanding of the transactional relationships between living human beings and their environments" (p. 42).

Drawing on Hannah Arendt's understanding of praxis, Greene (1988) argues that the "consequences of free action . . . are to a large degree unpredictable" (p. 46). Engaging in our best practical intelligence is "the price we must pay" for democratic pluralism (p. 46). Millgram (1997) describes Aristotle's ideal of practical intelligence as decision making "informed by the full range of considerations" (p. 53). This is the understanding of intelligence that accompanies Greene's inquiry into human freedom. She has faith that humans can help one another cultivate a sophisticated "critical" deliberation (Greene, 1988, p. 4). She cites Dewey on this point: "Social conditions interact with the preferences of an individual—in a way favorable to actualizing freedom only when they develop intelligence, not abstract knowledge and abstract thought, but power of vision and reflection. For these take effect in making preference, desire, and purpose more flexible, alert, and resolute" (p. 4).

Finally, Greene (1988) argues for a subtle "dialectical" understanding of human freedom, in which critical concerns for freedom's constraints are balanced by considerations of human development. In her overview of American discourse practices on "human freedom," she notes that this dialectical sensibility was particularly well articulated by John Dewey:

> Dewey . . . grew up in the Hegelian stream; and the Hegelian view of dialectical change and development remained alive in his thinking. What he rejected in time, however, was the idea of the World Spirit, the Absolute, the cosmic order. . . . The Hegelian view that autonomy and freedom are attained when human beings grasp, through the exercise of reason, the overarching order of things was revised. For Dewey, there was no cosmic purpose fulfilling itself in history. Nonetheless, there was a clear connection between identity and what he called the "freed intelligence" necessary for direction of freedom of action. (pp. 42–43)

Greene's *The Dialectic of Freedom* is essentially a careful analysis and poetic evocation of this "freed intelligence." Through numerous illustrations, descriptions, and metaphors, she presents her understanding of democratically liberated consciousness. To acknowledge the dialectical implications of her philosophical inquiry, she continuously acknowledges both the "negative" and "positive" poles of her presentation. She uses these terms descriptively, as a physicist would. Negative freedom is not "negative" in a moral sense, nor is positive freedom "positive" in a moral sense. Negative and positive struggles are, simply, two sides of the same "emancipatory" coin. Negative freedom refers to the deliberate rejection of "oppression or exploitation or segregation or neglect" (Greene, 1988, p. 9). Without a critical sense of negative freedom, people remain anchored, submerged, or even rootless. They lack an awareness of their psychological and/or social limitations.[2] Negative freedom connotes "the right not to be interfered with or coerced or compelled to do what [one] did not choose to do" (p. 16). In contrast, positive freedom refers to expressions of "self-direction." The critical norm of positive freedom "suggests that freedom shows itself or comes into being when individuals come together in a particular way, when they are authentically present to one another (without masks, pretenses, badges of office), when they have a project they can mutually pursue" (Greene, 1988, pp. 16–17).

Greene's (1988) discussion of negative and positive freedom is quite comprehensive and diversified. She describes a variety of forms of oppression, exploitation, segregation, and neglect in American society. Included are not only those associated with racial, gender, and class relations, but more subtle forms such as "constraining family rituals," "bureaucratic supervisory systems," and, ironically, even freedom as a media "icon" that benefits the wealthy (Greene, 1988, p. 17). She recognizes that struggles against freedom's constraints must be broad-based and multileveled.

Greene's (1988) analysis of positive liberatory endeavors is equally sophisticated. Tapping into American history, she draws on expressions of positive freedom from the writings of Thomas Jefferson, Mark Twain, Horace Mann, Ralph Waldo Emerson, Henry David Thoreau, Nathaniel Hawthorne, Herman Melville, Walt Whitman, Jane Addams, Emily Dickinson, W. E. B. DuBois, Martin Luther King, Virginia Woolf, Joan Didion, Alice Walker, Walker Percy, among many others. She summarizes these expressions of "positive" human freedom as follows:

> Looking back, we can discern individuals in their we-relations with others, inserting themselves in the world by means of projects, embarking on new beginnings in spaces they open themselves. We can recall them—Thomas Jefferson, the Grimke sisters, Susan B. Anthony, Jane Addams, Frederick Douglass, W. E. B. DuBois, Martin Luther King, John Dewey, Carol Gilligan,

Nel Noddings, Mary Daly—opening spaces where freedom is the mainspring, where people create themselves by acting in concert. (p. 134)

From the beginning sentences in her book, Maxine Greene is careful to stay critically positioned within the negative/positive dialectic of freedom. She continuously wants to acknowledge both constraints and possibilities and, in doing so, she wants to affirm the intimate relationship between personal and social liberation. In the opening sentences of her introduction, she writes:

This book arises out of a lifetime's preoccupation with quest, with pursuit. On the one hand, the quest has been deeply personal: that of a woman striving to affirm the feminine as wife, mother, and friend, while reaching, always reaching, beyond the limits imposed by the obligations of a woman's life. On the other hand, it has been in some sense deeply public as well: that of a person struggling to connect the undertaking of education, with which she has been so long involved, to the making and remaking of a public space, a space of dialogue and possibility. (p. xi)

THE ETHICS OF STRONG DEMOCRACY

Maxine Greene's inquiry into "human freedom" can be characterized as the philosophical study of "strong" democracy, which Barber (1984) defines as follows:

Strong democracy is a distinctively modern form of participatory democracy. It rests on the idea of a self-governing community of citizens who are united less by homogeneous interests than by civic education and who are made capable of common purpose and mutual action by virtue of their civic attitudes and participatory institutions rather than their altruism or their good nature. Strong democracy is consonant with—indeed it depends upon—the politics of conflict, the sociology of pluralism, and the separation of private and public realms of action. It is not intrinsically inimical to either the size or the technology of modern society and is therefore wedded neither to antiquarian republicanism nor to face-to-face parochialism. Yet it challenges the politics of elites and masses that masquerades as democracy in the West and in doing so offers a relevant alternative to what we have called thin democracy—that is, to instrumental, representative, liberal democracy. (p. 117)

An *ethics of strong democracy* can be gleaned from Maxine Greene's study of "human freedom," and the articulation of this ethics helps provide a concrete normative framework for the practice of democratic curriculum leadership. Four ethical principles can be identified as central to Greene's philosophical discussion. *First of all, the strong democrat engages in a continuous, lifelong dialogical inquiry that deepens her/his understanding of the interdependence of all living things.* Greene (1988) writes that what we should seek is "freedom developed by human beings who have acted to make a space for themselves in the presence of others" (p. 56). Over a lifetime of growth-oriented activity, the *strong* democrat cultivates a deep sense of the interconnectedness of life. Garrison (1997) describes this feeling of interconnectedness as a multiperspective (or perspectival) view of reality:

> Finite creatures can grow wiser only if they share perspectives, for seeing things from the standpoint of others also allows us to multiply perspectives. That is why Dewey thought dialogues across differences were essential for those who desire to grow. When a single standpoint excludes others, the result is a distorted view of reality. Monism is dogmatism. (p. 15)

As Odin (1996) notes, George Mead (1934) has developed a social psychology of "role taking" that is based on this perspectival feel for life. It is a view of the human individual as a "decentered multiple self" whereby "the *psyche* or soul is not an eternal oneness but an irreducible plurality" (Odin, 1996, p. 211). *Self* is understood as an identity construction that emerges out of a context of dialogue with diverse *others.* Odin (1996) expands:

> For Mead, *perspectivism* means the ability of an autonomous rational subject to take the role of others, or as it were, to enter into the perspective of others in the community. From the standpoint of this social perspectivism he thus recommends that ethical conduct be regulated by a procedure that he calls "role taking." This procedure requires that any free rational agent making an ethical judgment put himself into the position of all who would be affected if a particular norm were to take effect within a problematic situation. (pp. 240–241)

Second, the strong democrat seeks a multilayered understanding of curriculum practice. Deweyan democratic education cannot be described in simpleminded, technical terms. Lather (1996) critiques the penchant toward technical simplicity in educational inquiry: "Sometimes we need a density that fits the thoughts being expressed. In such places, clear and concise prose would be a sort of cheat tied to the anti-intellectualism rife in U.S. society that deskills readers" (p. 528).

Greene's (1988) position that human "reality" is a personally and socially constructed, multilayered phenomenon is a widely embraced tenet of current curriculum scholarship. Pinar and colleagues (1995) point out that this ontological commitment, which gathered momentum during the reconceptualization phase of curriculum studies, has resulted in a sophisticated, intertextual understanding of learning: "To understand educational experience requires being in the political, racial, aesthetic, spiritual, gendered, global, and phenomenological world" (p. 852). They note that this subtle feel for educational experience is "much more complicated than most politicians and many colleagues in arts and sciences realize" (p. 858) and points to "a political phenomenological understanding of curriculum, influenced by gender analysis, autobiographical theory, situated internationally in a multiracial global village" (p. 864). They then conclude that this understanding can lead to the maturation of an independent and autonomous field of curriculum study characterized by a Deweyan philosophical outlook:

> The intertextual understanding of curriculum that the reconceptualized field offers can lead us to ask with greater complexity and sophistication, the traditional curriculum questions: what knowledge is of most worth? What do we make of the world we have been given, and how shall we remake ourselves to give birth to a new social order? What John Dewey said in reference to philosophy might be said in reference to the contemporary curriculum field: "A [curriculum theory] which was conscious of its own business and province would then perceive that it is an intellectualized wish, an aspiration subject to rational discriminations and tests, a social hope reduced to a working program of action, a prophecy of the future, but one disciplined by serious thought and knowledge" (Dewey [1919/1982], quoted in Westbrook, 1991, p. 147).
>
> Here Dewey unites self-realization and society (Westbrook, 1991), two of the major currents in contemporary curriculum scholarship. An intellectualized wish expressed as a social practice, thoroughly theorized and subject to rigorous critique which functions to reformulate the wish, re-expressed as practice: a moving form, that is understanding curriculum today. (Pinar et al., 1995, p. 866)

The *strong* democrat works with this understanding of curriculum.

Third, the strong democrat engages in a sophisticated holistic deliberative educational practice. As noted earlier, Snauwaert (1993) characterizes the Deweyan understanding of democracy and education as a *developmental* outlook on the "good" life. He then notes that this philosophical orientation is guided by a sophisticated and holistic feel for human growth: "Development, in this tradition, is conceived broadly as the all-around growth of the individual, which may include the development of moral, intellectual, spiritual, and creative capacities" (Snauwaert, 1993, p. 5).

The *strong* democratic educator continuously reflects on the specifics of any particular educational practice in relationship to this broad, holistic sense of human growth. Short (1991) provides a general overview of this type of reflection:

> It is possible for intellectual convenience to analyze something or attend only to one part of a phenomenon at a time, but in the real world of human activity everything that is done occurs as wholes and must be recognized as such. If we impose an analysis or partial perception on what presents itself to us, we do not grasp the reality accurately. Wholes are often difficult to understand, but we must know when we are dealing with whole entities and when we are mentally separating parts of the whole for clearer analysis. (p. 12)

Finally, the strong democrat engages in a continuous critical awareness of the complex dialectics of democratic emancipation. As noted in the analysis of *The Dialectic of Freedom,* Maxine Greene is careful to stay critically positioned within the negative/positive dynamics of human freedom. She continuously acknowledges both the constraints on, and possibilities of, democratic liberation, and, in doing so, she constantly refers to the intimate relationship between personal and social freedom. When she examines questions of human "emancipation," we know not only what she is *against* but what she is *for.*

Geuss (1981) identifies three characteristics of well-developed critical theories: they have an emancipatory focus, they posit a form of critical knowing, and they encourage reflection. Perhaps due to the influence of Karl Marx's critical theorizing, definitions of critically informed practice, or *praxis,* tend to focus on the exploitative economic and political dimensions of a culture. For example, Beyer and Apple (1988) write that praxis "involves not only the justifiable concern for reflective action, but thought and action combined and enlivened by a sense of power and politics" (p. 4). Marcuse (1969) points out the limitations of this type of critical work in consumer societies and argues for critical work on "the creation of an *aesthetic ethos*" (p. 24). He writes:

> [The causes of domination and servitude] are economic-political, but since they have shaped the very instincts and needs of men, no economic and political changes will bring this historical continuum to a stop unless they are carried through by men who are physiologically and psychologically able to experience things, and each other, outside the context of violence and exploitation. The new sensibility has become, by this very token, *praxis:* it emerges in the struggle against violence and exploitation where this struggle is waged for essentially new ways and forms of life: negation of the entire

Establishment, its morality, culture; affirmation of the right to build a society in which the abolition of poverty and toil terminates in a universe where the sensuous, the playful, the calm, and the beautiful become forms of existence and thereby the *Form* of the society itself. The aesthetic as the possible Form of a free society appears at that stage of development where the intellectual and material resources for the conquest of scarcity are available. (p. 25)

In the spirit of Marcuse's critically informed aesthetic sensibility, Greene (1988) presents an interpretation of praxis that reworks critical economic and political analysis into a humanistic aesthetics. She asks her readers to consider not only the overt, covert, and structurally embedded reasons why people do not live a life of *dialogical inquiry* but how progressive educators can encourage this way of living. The focus is not only on what is wrong but on how this wrong can be righted through educational activity. This understanding of praxis is "posthumanist" in its orientation. She acknowledges the importance of critical structural analysis but does not lose sight of the human capacity to create a meaningful life. Spanos (1993) describes a posthumanist curriculum in this way:

An oppositional pedagogical practice that takes place in the arena of crisis where power is unevenly distributed theoretically makes students aware of . . . their mastery of the Master, as it were—without falling into the trap of reinscribing them into . . . [a hegemonic] structure [from which they cannot escape]. . . . [Posthumanism] would enable a truly multicultural democracy, a democracy in which the differential voices always already risk their identities in dialogue. (p. 220)

THE PRACTICE OF DEMOCRATIC CURRICULUM LEADERSHIP

When the ethics of strong democracy is applied to the practice of curriculum leadership, a very specific and challenging *transformative* agenda emerges. The concept of "transformation" denotes fundamental, radical, and critically elevated change. The transformative reform agenda of the democratic curriculum leader possesses five interrelated dimensions. *First of all, the democratic curriculum leader seeks ways to introduce and support teaching for authentic inquiry learning.* The focus is not on how to raise students' standardized test scores but on how to facilitate a personal and collaborative search for a meaningful life. As quoted earlier, Greene (1988) describes this instructional orientation as being "authentically present to one another (without masks, pretenses, badges of office)" (pp. 16–17).

The democratic curriculum leader helps teachers finds ways to en-

gage their students in personal *meaning making* through passionate inquiry projects. Although this *constructivist* education (to use the current
progressive, "best practice" term) often results in the achievement of high
standardized test scores, this is not the goal of this type of instruction.
The purpose is not to attain particular managerial mandates but to assist
students in the realization of a life of authentic inquiry.

Given the politics of a particular educational setting and the dominance of the curriculum management paradigm, the democratic curriculum leader may be required to "package" his/her instructional leadership
activities in standardized achievement terms. Anxious parents may need
to be reassured that their children's authentic learning will not prevent
them from competing in a meritocratic society. This reassurance will require the democratic curriculum leader to engage in a "bordercrossing"
(Giroux, 1992) between the managerial and democratic outlook on life.

*Second, the democratic curriculum leader seeks ways to introduce and support
teacher-led professional development.* Teaching for authentic inquiry learning
is a very sophisticated form of instructional work that can be actualized
only through ongoing inquiry. Teachers must become practitioners-
scholars-professionals who are willing to engage in a career of continuing
study in a collegial context.

Lieberman (1989) describes this context as a "professional culture"
that is characterized by trust building among all participants through an
open examination of personal-professional beliefs, by continuing collaborative inquiry into the conduct and improvement of schooling, and by
confronting top-down power relationships. Sirotnik (1989) argues that
schools must no longer be targets of others' reform agendas. Schools must
become vital "centers" of change—places where those who daily provide
the educational services have the time and energy to decide how best to
conduct their professional lives. Senge (1990) delineates three general
strategies for creating a "learning" organization: (1) supporting workers'
abilities to shape their professional future, (2) using creative tension between visions and reality to stimulate growth, and (3) encouraging systems thinking—helping people see interrelationships, not simplistic cause
and effect patterns.

*Third, the democratic curriculum leader seeks ways to redesign educational
programs so that they are properly supportive of teaching for authentic inquiry
learning and collegial professional development.* Providing leadership for
curriculum design deliberations is a challenging but necessary feature
of the democratic curriculum leader's transformative agenda. As Walker
(1971, 1990) documents, program redesign deliberations require extensive consensus building around common beliefs and purposes (the co-
construction of a curricular "platform"), collaborative discussions over ed-

ucational solutions to shared problems, and collective decisions on particular program designs.

Curriculum redesign deliberations can be tedious and politically demanding. However, this work is essential to the realization of a professional learning culture. Most teachers are not willing to alter their instructional behaviors unless they feel that their inquiry efforts are programmatically supported (Paris, 1993). If their daily work life is structured by pupil performance objectives, scope and sequence charts, textbook acquisitions, and standardized tests, why should they change? Why should they reflect on how to facilitate authentic inquiry learning? After all, this is a very demanding way to teach, and what's the point of fighting the instructional management system? If democratic curriculum leaders want to support teachers' continuing study of authentic inquiry learning, they must help create educational programs that foster the "expressive outcomes" associated with this type of education (Eisner, 1994b). They must help establish an instructional context that provides for alternatives to standardized goals and assessments.

Fourth, the democratic curriculum leader seeks ways to redesign organizational structures so that they properly support collegial professional development. Organizational redesign is equally as important as programmatic redesign. Democratic curriculum leaders cannot expect most teachers to become active participants in a learning community collegium unless the teachers feel that their collaborative inquiry efforts will be organizationally supported (Paris, 1993). Again, from a pragmatic standpoint, few teachers will be willing to work against the structures of a top-down, or "power over" (Kreisberg, 1992), management system.

Organizational development (OD) work is similar to program redesign activities. Schmuck and Runkel (1985) describe two essential phases of OD. In phase I, the focus is on training members of the organization to examine how they communicate, resolve conflicts, and express trust and regard toward each other. The goal is to create a sense of collegial identity within the institution. In phase II, the goal is to develop the analytical and critical aspects of professional community life. Teachers and other important curriculum stakeholders work to identify common beliefs and concerns, critically assess the overt and covert meanings of their organizational life, and plan ways to create institutional structures that support collaborative professional inquiry. As Sergiovanni (1992) notes, this reform work can result in the creation of a shared pedagogical vision, which he characterizes as an organizational *covenant:*

> When purpose, social contract, and local school autonomy become the basis
> of schooling, two important things happen. The school is transformed from

an organization to a covenantal community, and the basis of authority changes, from an emphasis on bureaucratic and psychological authority to moral authority. To put it another way, the school changes from a secular organization to a sacred organization, from a mere instrument designed to achieve certain ends to a virtuous enterprise. (p. 102)

Finally, the democratic curriculum leader seeks ways to establish meaningful school–community dialogue on the transformative efforts. As noted earlier, the reform work of the democratic curriculum leader involves fundamental, critically elevated change. Teachers are encouraged to focus on their students' authentic inquiry learning, not on their standardized test scores. Teachers are asked to become active, responsible participants of a professional collegium, not loyal union members or efficient followers of state and local instructional management decisions. To achieve these lofty goals, educational programs must be redesigned, and organizational structures must be altered. In most settings, such dramatic reform is not possible without a carefully cultivated dialogue among all *curriculum stakeholders:* educational administrators, teachers, teacher aides, students, students' parents, school psychologists, social workers, community, business, and religious leaders, and so on. Any one of these interest groups can limit, damage, and perhaps even undermine the transformative efforts.

Democratic curriculum leaders must understand that their work has an *ecological* or *systemic* dimension. Considering this critical feature of fundamental change, Eisner (1994a) writes:

The reform of education not only requires deeper and more comprehensive analysis of schools; it must also attend to the dimensions of schooling that must be collectively addressed to make educational reform educationally real. This attention must go well beyond changes in individual aspects of educational practice. . . . Applied to schools, it means that the school as a whole must be addressed. What we are dealing with is the creation of a culture. In many ways the word culture is especially apt. A culture in the biological sense is a set of living organisms that can grow only if the medium in which they reside is hospitable to their growth. The school is that medium. The culture is the students and the adults who work with them. The growth we seek is the enlargement of mind. To create the medium they need, we need to pay attention to matters of mix. What goes into that mix surely includes the intentions that give direction to the enterprise, the structure that supports it, the curriculum that provides its content, the teaching with which that content is mediated, and the evaluation system that enables us to monitor and improve its operation. No educational reform that has been proposed has collectively addressed these primary dimensions of schooling. To approach the reform of schools ecologically or, as others put it, systemically, requires, at the very least, attention to intentions—what aims really matter in the educational enterprise as a whole? (pp. 10–11)

THE CONTINUING CRITICAL STUDY OF DEMOCRATIC CURRICULUM LEADERSHIP

Democratic curriculum leadership is a very complex undertaking. It is informed by a "holistic" vision of a caring learning community that is quite complex in its details. Individuals who have both the opportunity and the desire to engage in this challenging transformative work, will need to become dedicated students of their reform practices. The practice of democratic curriculum leadership cannot be translated into five, or 10, or even 20 easy steps. There is simply too much to learn and too many historical, cultural, developmental, instructional, programmatic, organizational, and political subtleties to address.

The continuing critical study of democratic curriculum leadership will need to proceed on two simultaneous fronts. First, there are the pressing details of the daily reform activities. Curriculum leaders will need to address such questions as the following:

- How can our mathematics teacher, Mr. Smith, be introduced to the latest progressive thinking about teaching his discipline through hands-on, problem-solving activities?
- How can our middle school teacher, Ms. Fuentes, be encouraged to lead a study group of teachers on the progressive topic of writing as a process?
- How can we revamp our social studies program to facilitate student inquiry into current community issues?
- How can our high school teachers spend more quality collaborative inquiry time with one another?
- How do we organize a school–community town meeting to address concerns over low test scores in the sciences?

While immersed in these daily reform details, the democratic curriculum leader must be careful not to lose sight of what this reform is all about. When walking among the "trees," the democratic curriculum leader must not lose sight of the "forest." In this case, the "forest" is the holistic vision of a *caring, collaborative learning community.* Maintaining this balance between "forest" and "trees" is not possible without establishing a rhythm between attention to the details of curricular change and continuing *critical reflection* on the "big picture" of this reform effort. To facilitate this rhythm, four critical topics have been selected from the tradition of curriculum studies: *curriculum deliberation, reflexive systems, cultural criticism* and *educational mythopoetics.* Before introducing these four critical topics, a brief overview of contemporary curriculum studies will provide a context for this discussion.

The field of curriculum studies was introduced earlier in this chapter, and it was pointed out that, beginning in 1969, the field was "reconceptualized" (Pinar, 1975) to focus on a diverse set of critical projects. Between 1969 and the present, curriculum scholars have engaged in numerous types of curriculum inquiry on a wide variety of curricular problems. Two books provide an overview of this diversified critical work. Short (1991) introduces 17 types of curriculum inquiry, which are defined as processes "designed to answer a certain class of previously unanswered questions. Any such process is comprised of a series of proven procedures for making and justifying knowledge claims or obtaining answers to such questions that are congruent with some theory of inquiry" (p. 14). Pinar, Reynolds, Slattery, and Taubman (1995) introduce hundreds of specific critical curriculum study projects, which they collectively characterize as the "mosaic . . . [or] complicated symphony that is the curriculum study field" (p. 5).

Within the context of this curriculum study "symphony," four projects have been selected to facilitate the continuing study of *democratic curriculum leadership.* Two main characteristics identify these projects as "critical."[3] First, they are each informed by an emancipatory interest that is linked to *democracy as a moral way of life.* Each project identifies a way of becoming "democratically liberated" through a particular type of knowing. Second, they each present a way to engage in reflective practice. Each project provides specific guidance on how its "liberatory knowing" can be used by thoughtful practitioners.

In Chapter 3, Gail McCutcheon will present the topic of *curriculum deliberation.* Her emancipatory focus is on how to free educators and their students from top-down management mandates through on-site collaborative decision making. In Chapter 4, Noel Gough will present the topic of *reflexive systems.* His liberatory interest is on how to free educators and their students from the limited, linear rationality of bureaucratic planning and control (the paradigm of scientific management) through systems thinking informed by chaos, complexity, and narrative theory. In Chapter 5, Joe Kincheloe will present the topic of *cultural criticism.* His emancipatory interest is on how to free educators and their students from social injustices and subjugation through radical democratic critique. In Chapter 6, Kathleen Kesson will present the topic of *educational mythopoetics.* Her emancipatory focus is on how to free educators and their students from alienating curriculum discourse through the exercise of their open-hearted, poetic imaginations.

After presenting an overview of their critical topic, each chapter author will provide specific guidance on how his/her form of "emancipatory knowing" can be used to reflect on the practice of democratic curriculum leadership. To facilitate this "practical" feature of critical work, a particular procedure was followed. A study group of eight democratic curriculum leaders in the state of Vermont was organized. Each chapter author prepared an essay introducing the particular curriculum study topic. The Vermont study group read and critically discussed each essay. Questions, difficulties, and issues of application were raised. These practitioner-based discussions were videotaped, and the videotapes were sent to each chapter author, who then used the critical feedback to make final revisions to the chapters. Although this procedure was followed consistently by all four chapter authors, Chapter 6 is unique in that Kathleen Kesson lives in Vermont and therefore was able to establish a closer dialogical relationship with each study group member. Her chapter is, therefore, slightly longer than the other three and is written in a more personal, interactive style.

The members of the study group will be introduced in Chapter 2, and this introduction will include background information on the progressive policy context in which they work. Additional details on the educational environment in Vermont have been incorporated into Chapter 6. Chapter 7, the concluding chapter of this book, will include three personal reflections on the practice and continuing study of democratic curriculum leadership. The first two reflections are composed by Jim Henderson and Kathleen Kesson, the book's co-editors; the final reflection is written by Kerrin McCadden, who is a member of the Vermont study group. These personal reflections are an appropriate way to conclude this text because the political work of Deweyan democracy is highly personal in nature. The placement of Kerrin's reflection, as the final contribution, is symbolically significant. It stresses the importance of the day-to-day practical work of democratic curriculum leadership by positioning a *practitioner,* not a *theoretician,* as the individual who has the final word in this book.

THE HERMENEUTIC STUDY OF DEMOCRATIC CURRICULUM LEADERSHIP

Now that the practice of democratic curriculum leadership and the four curriculum topics that will be used to facilitate the *continuing critical study* of this practice have been introduced, attention can be directed to the challenge of functioning as a career-long student of this very sophisticated form of transformative educational work.

As mentioned above, while immersed in her/his daily reform activities, the democratic curriculum leader must be careful not to lose sight of what this reform is all about—the holistic vision of a *caring, learning community*. Attention must shift continuously between the details of the practice and the "big picture" of this reform effort. This understanding of reflective practice, or praxis, is informed by the tradition of *hermeneutic inquiry*. Smith (1991) provides a concise account of this form of inquiry:

> The hermeneutic imagination constantly asks for what is at work in particular ways of speaking and acting in order to facilitate an ever-deepening appreciation of that wholeness and integrity of the world which must be present for thought and action to be possible at all. . . . The hermeneutic modus has more the character of conversation than, say, of analysis and the trumpeting of truth claims. When one is engaged in a good conversation, there is a certain quality of self-forgetfulness as one gives oneself over to the conversation itself, so that the truth that is realized in the conversation is never the possession of any one of the speakers or camps, but rather is something that all concerned realize they share in together. This is a point well stated by Thomas Merton: (1961). "If I give you my truth but do not receive your truth in return, then there can be no truth between us." The conversational quality of hermeneutic truth points to the requirement that any study carried on in the name of hermeneutics should provide a report of the [student's] own transformations undergone in the process of the inquiry; a showing of the dialogical journey, we might call it. (pp. 197–198)

This book has been organized to facilitate the "dialogical journey" of democratic curriculum leaders. Each critical study topic presents a "truth" about the holistic intent of this leadership approach. Each chapter in this book provides insight into, and a unique perspective on, the meaning of a *caring, collaborative learning community*. This book is designed to facilitate continuous professional growth characterized as the *hermeneutic circle*—the continuous reflection on the details of practice in light of selected critical theorizing and, reciprocally, the continuous critique of the critical theorizing in light of practical experience. In a nutshell, this book has been written to foster the *hermeneutic understanding* of democratic curriculum leadership. It is designed to encourage a cyclical *rhythm* between progressive, transformative activity and a diversified critical reflection.

The concluding chapter will return to this hermeneutic theme. It will serve as a final statement on the continuing study challenges that are embedded in the practice of democratic curriculum leadership.

NOTES

1. For an analysis of the pragmatic purposes of the Tyler Rationale, see P. S. Hlebowitsh, *Radical Curriculum Theory Reconsidered: A Historical Approach* (New York: Teachers College Press, 1993).

2. In classical Marxian terms, they possess false consciousness.

3. For a more in-depth discussion of the central characteristics of "critical" work, see R. Geuss, *The Idea of a Critical Theory* (Cambridge: Cambridge University Press, 1981), B. Fay, *Critical Social Science: Liberation and Its Limits* (Ithaca, NY: Cornell University Press, 1987), and J. Kincheloe, *Teachers as Researchers: Qualitative Inquiry as a Path to Empowerment* (London: Falmer, 1991).

REFERENCES

Barber, B. R. (1984). *Strong democracy: Participatory politics for a new age.* Berkeley: University of California Press.

Beyer, L. (1996). Teachers' reflections on the struggle for democratic classrooms. *Teaching Education, 8*(1), 91–102.

Beyer, L. E., & Apple, M. W. (1988). Values and politics in the curriculum. In L. E. Beyer & M. W. Apple (Eds.), *Curriculum: Problems, politics, and possibilities* (pp. 3–16). Albany: State University of New York Press.

Bobbitt, F. (1918). *The curriculum.* Boston: Houghton Mifflin.

Carlson, D. (1997). *Making progress: Education and culture in new times.* New York: Teachers College Press.

Dewey, J. (1916). *Democracy and education.* New York: Macmillan.

Dewey, J. (1963). *Experience and education.* New York: Collier Books. (Original work published 1938)

Dewey, J. (1982). Philosophy and democracy. In J. A. Boydston (Ed.), *The middle works of John Dewey, 1899–1924* (Vol. 11, pp. 41–53). Carbondale: Southern Illinois University Press. (Original work published 1919)

Dewey, J. (1989). *Freedom and culture.* Buffalo, NY: Prometheus. (Original work published 1939)

Eisner, E. W. (1994a). *Cognition and curriculum reconsidered* (2nd ed.). New York: Teachers College Press.

Eisner, E. W. (1994b). *The educational imagination: On the design and evaluation of school programs* (3rd ed.). New York: Macmillan.

Gadamer, H. (1975). *Philosophical hermeneutics* (D. E. Linge, Ed. & Trans.). Berkeley: University of California Press.

Garrison, J. (1997). *Dewey and Eros: Wisdom and desire in the art of teaching.* New York: Teachers College Press.

Geuss, R. (1981). *The idea of a critical theory.* Cambridge: Cambridge University Press.

Giroux, H. A. (1992). *Bordercrossings.* New York: Routledge.

Greene, M. (1988). *The dialectic of freedom.* New York: Teachers College Press.

Jackson, P. W. (1992). Conceptions of curriculum and curriculum specialists. In P. W. Jackson (Ed.), *Handbook of research on curriculum* (pp. 3–40). New York: Macmillan.

Kreisberg, S. (1992). *Transforming power: Domination, empowerment, and education.* Albany: State University of New York Press.

Lather, P. (1996). Troubling clarity: The politics of accessible language. *Harvard Educational Review, 66*(3), 525–545.

Lieberman, A. (Ed.). (1989). *Building a professional culture in schools.* New York: Teachers College Press.

Marcuse, H. (1969). *An essay on liberation.* Boston: Beacon Press.

Maxcy, S. J. (1991). *Educational leadership: A critical pragmatic perspective.* New York: Bergin & Garvey.

Mead, G. H. (1934). *Mind, self & society* (C. W. Morris, Ed.). Chicago: University of Chicago Press.

Merton, T. (1961). *Emblems of a season of fury.* Norfolk: New Directions.

Millgram, E. (1997). *Practical induction.* Cambridge, MA: Harvard University Press.

Odin, S. (1996). *The social self in Zen and American pragmatism.* Albany: State University of New York Press.

Paris, C. L. (1993). *Teacher agency and curriculum making in classrooms.* New York: Teachers College Press.

Pinar, W. F. (Ed.). (1975). *Curriculum theorizing: The reconceptualists.* Berkeley: McCutchan.

Pinar, W. F., Reynolds, W. M., Slattery, P., & Taubman, P. M. (1995). *Understanding curriculum: An introduction to the study of historical and contemporary curriculum discourses.* New York: Peter Lang.

Plato. (trans. 1956). *The republic* (B. Jowett, Trans.). New York: Modern Library.

Schmuck, R., & Runkel, P. (1985). *The handbook of organization development in schools* (3rd ed.). Prospect Heights, IL: Waveland Press.

Schubert, W. H. (1986). *Curriculum: Perspective, paradigm, and possibility.* New York: Macmillan.

Senge, P. M. (1990). *The fifth discipline: The art and practice of the learning organization.* New York: Bantam Books.

Sergiovanni, T. J. (1992). *Moral leadership: Getting to the heart of school improvement.* San Francisco: Jossey-Bass.

Short, E. C. (Ed.). (1991). *Forms of curriculum inquiry.* Albany: State University of New York Press.

Sirotnik, K. A. (1989). The school as the center of change. In T. J. Sergiovanni & J. H. Moore (Eds.), *Schooling for tomorrow: Directing reforms to issues that count* (pp. 89–113). Boston: Allyn & Bacon.

Smith, D. G. (1991). Hermeneutic inquiry: The hermeneutic imagination and the pedagogic text. In E. C. Short (Ed.), *Forms of curriculum inquiry* (pp. 187–209). Albany: State University of New York Press.

Snauwaert, D. T. (1993). *Democracy, education, and governance: A developmental conception.* Albany: State University of New York Press.

Spanos, W. V. (1993). *The end of education: Toward humanism.* Minneapolis: University of Minnesota Press.

Tyler, R. W. (1949). *Basic principles of curriculum and instruction.* Chicago: University of Chicago Press.

Walker, D. F. (1971). A naturalistic model for curriculum development. *School Review, 80*(1), 51–69.

Walker, D. F. (1990). *Fundamentals of curriculum.* New York: Harcourt Brace Jovanovich.

Westbrook, R. B. (1991). *John Dewey and American democracy.* Ithaca, NY: Cornell University Press.

The Practice and Critical Study of Democratic Curriculum Leadership

KATHLEEN R. KESSON

IN THIS CHAPTER, we introduce the Vermont curriculum leaders who formed the study group that read and critiqued the curriculum study topics that will be presented in Chapters 3–6. We open with a brief description of the sociocultural context in which they work. We will then present some of the stories that have shaped their professional lives and reform efforts. These narratives will reveal some common experiences and commitments that have shaped who they are as Vermont democratic curriculum leaders.

While sharing their "war stories," the study group gradually established a *culture of inquiry,* which enabled them to safely explore the complex and controversial ideas associated with the four critical curriculum topics. The level of analysis and critique engendered by their collaborative dialogue is demonstrated particularly in the closing chapter of the book, in which Kerrin McCadden, one of the members of the study group, reflects upon her practice in light of this text's critical hermeneutic framework. It is our ultimate hope that you, the readers of this book, will be encouraged to engage in a similar kind of critical analysis of your curriculum reform efforts.

THE VERMONT EDUCATIONAL CONTEXT

Vermont, a small New England state, is known for its democratic tradition of town meetings, picture postcard landscapes, long winters, maple syrup,

Understanding Democratic Curriculum Leadership. Copyright © 1999 by Teachers College, Columbia University. All rights reserved. ISBN 0-8077-3826-3 (pbk), ISBN 0-8077-3827-1 (cloth). Prior to photocopying items for classroom use, please contact the Copyright Clearance Center, Customer Service, 222 Rosewood Dr., Danvers, MA 01923, USA, tel. (508) 750-8400.

Ben and Jerry's ice cream, and progressive politics. (Progressives have long been influential in Burlington city politics, and Vermont's one representative to the United States Congress is an independent socialist.) The strong civic culture in Vermont was highlighted recently in a study by Tom W. Rice and Alexander F. Sumberg (1997), in which they looked at the relationship between civic culture and government performance, and rated the states of the United States accordingly. The elements of a strong civic culture that these researchers looked at included *civic engagement,* or the extent to which citizens participate in public affairs and promote the public good; *political equality,* or the extent to which relations between individuals in public, and most private, spheres are horizontal and cooperative; *solidarity, trust, and tolerance,* the extent to which there is fellowship and toleration of a wide range of ideas and lifestyles; and *social structures of cooperation,* or the extent to which there exists a dense, interlocking web of social organization. The conclusion of the study was that states that are more civic tend to have governments that enact more liberal and innovative policies, and are more effective in governance. Vermont scored the highest of all the states in terms of civic culture.

The state is home to a mostly rural population with a large number of artists, writers, intellectuals, and entrepreneurs as well as farmers and loggers. A strong environmental ethic is indicated by the fact that Vermont has moved from being three-quarters deforested at one time to its current situation of being three-quarters forest and woodland. To a large degree, the state is dependent on environmental and historic preservation for its economic well-being, and tourists for some time have provided a major source of income for the inhabitants. The folks who live here have a Yankee reputation for hard work, thrift, both individualism and neighborliness, and independent judgment.

Through the years, Vermont has sustained a strong commitment to the local control of schools, a commitment perhaps related to both the independent spirit of Vermonters and the tradition of face-to-face democracy still found in town meetings here. There is an aversion to external educational mandates, which is reflected in the relative autonomy that districts, schools, and teachers have. There is no statewide textbook adoption process, for example, no state-mandated standardized tests, and no common curriculum. It is perhaps this relative independence, along with a moderately friendly climate for experimentation, that has resulted in Vermont's reputation for being in the forefront of educational innovation. Portfolio assessment, for example, was pioneered here, both in K–12 schools and in teacher licensure. Vermont is also one of the first states to attempt to equalize state education funding, currently one of the hottest political topics here (in addition to being a Vermont version of a class war, the intense controversy is related to the clash of two deeply held and, in this case, contradictory civic interests: on the one hand, a commitment to local control, and on the other, a commitment to political equality). This climate of innovation, and the traditions of local control and face-to-face democracy, are important aspects of contemporary curriculum developments in the state.

These unique characteristics have not been enough to shelter Vermont from the larger forces of national educational politics. Like other states, it has responded to the "Nation at Risk" and "Goals 2000" imperatives with a flurry of activity intended to upgrade the expectations and the outcomes of its public education system. In the early 1990s, a series of conversations took place in focus forums across the state, which culminated in the development and publication of the Vermont Common Core of Learning. True to Vermont's town meeting tradition, the focus forums represented the effort to include as many interested Vermonters as possible in the discussion of "what every child should know and be able to do in the 21st century."

The *Vermont Common Core of Learning* was a simple, reader-friendly document that proposed four groups of "Vital Results" hoped for in learning: Reasoning and Problem-Solving, Communication, Personal Development, and Social Responsibility. The outcomes (21 altogether) were quite general and certainly would guarantee the autonomy of Vermont schools and the control over curriculum that teachers and local administrators had enjoyed for years. The outcomes also reflected a progressive perspective, embodying commitments to environmental protection, the eradication of racism and other forms of bias, the appreciation of cultural diversity, and the development of critical thinking.

Since the publication of the first draft of the *Common Core,* subsequent efforts have brought increased specificity to the original items generated by citizens. Responding to criticism about the "lack of content" in the *Common Core,* three commissions were formed to represent "Fields of Knowledge": Science, Math, and Technology; Arts, Language, and Literature; and History and Social Sciences. The commissions, with representation from higher education, elementary and secondary teachers and administrators, State Department of Education bureaucrats and policy makers, and some business leaders, were charged with the task of identifying essential knowledge and skills in the Fields of Knowledge and for the Vital Results, and with the development of standards gleaned from a review of the national standards in the various disciplines. Overseeing the work of the commissions was a Steering Committee, a similarly representative group. The work of the commissions finally (after numerous drafts and revisions) was synthesized by this latter group into *Vermont's Frame-*

work of Standards and Learning Opportunities, a 23-page document accompanied by a 33-page "how-to" guide, and was approved by the State Board of Education in January 1996. As of this writing, the *Framework* is in its implementation phase, accompanied by a variety of professional development activities as well as district- and building-level strategic planning and restructuring initiatives.

True to the democratic spirit in Vermont, the *Framework* has not been mandated. In reality, although many districts are formulating their own local frameworks based on the state document, it does provide a coherent set of guidelines for curriculum work in the state. In all of the conversations with the curriculum leaders who formed the study group for this book, the *Framework* was an absent presence, signifying its powerful force in the lives of all of those who work in education: teachers, administrators, teacher educators. And, due to fairly substantive public relations efforts, it is familiar to people outside of education as well: parents, community members, business leaders.

There has been controversy and conflict over the *Framework.* It has caused excitement, optimism, and enthusiasm, as well as confusion, indifference, and anger. It certainly has sparked dialogue and debate, which is perhaps one of its greatest accomplishments. Dewey (1938/1963) notes that "all social movements involve conflicts which are represented intellectually in controversies. It would not be a sign of health if such an important social interest as education were not also an arena of struggles, practical and theoretical" (p. 5). Whether one is supportive or dismissive of the *Framework,* or anywhere in between, it would be hard not to agree that it has expanded radically the possibilities for what goes on in classrooms. It is interdisciplinary, learner-centered, inquiry-based, constructivist, and friendly to progressive pedagogies. The extent to which these curriculum reform potentials have been realized varies widely across the state. While some districts and buildings are forging ahead with experiments and new initiatives, the *Framework* already gathers dust on some shelves. Whether the progressive possibilities of the *Framework* are actualized probably depends on the extent to which educators succumb to current technical and managerial initiatives around "standards" and "accountability" that unfortunately have begun to overshadow earlier concerns with issues of equity, social justice, and human development.

We chose to bring together a group of Vermont curriculum leaders for this book because of the unique educational context represented by the state. Many local factors work in favor of the development of democratic curriculum leadership: Vermont is small in scale, thus favorable to innovation, experimentation, and the distribution of information; it has a tradition of "strong democracy" and the local control of schools; it has, as mentioned above, a thriving civic culture; there is at least a stated agreement to top-down/bottom-up school reform; relationships between the education bureaucracy, public schools, and higher education are more cordial than in many other places; and the state now has a curriculum framework that provides a supportive "umbrella" for progressive pedagogies.

THE VERMONT STUDY GROUP

The particular participants chosen for this project represent a combined wealth of experience in teaching and administration. All of them share a commitment to a particular set of ethical positions: equity and fairness for all learners, constructivist practice, a student-centered curriculum, and democratic curriculum leadership. Some names have been changed to protect the identities of the participants.

- Carol Spencer has been both a foreign language teacher at the secondary level and a principal in three schools, and has, as she says, spent "20 years finding ways to help early adolescents access school knowledge."
- Mary Lyn Riggs was a high school teacher and middle school teacher for 15 years, and has been a principal for the past 12 years in both rural and suburban schools. She has a strong commitment to parent and community involvement and to the creation of a caring community for all learners.
- Carol Smith has been a middle grades, multiage teacher for 21 years, with a "focus on engaging students in all the decisions that need to be made around their education and the management of the classroom." She recently was named "Teacher of the Year" for her commitment to innovation and a student-centered curriculum.
- Jude Newman has been a classroom teacher, a gifted and talented coordinator, and the curriculum coordinator for a school district. She is currently the principal of an elementary school and believes strongly that "every child should have experiences with the gifted and talented teachers."
- Sarah Mohler taught seventh and eighth grades for many years, and has been a curriculum director for a supervisory union. She was active in the statewide middle grades initiative, as well as participating in the development of the *Framework*.
- Kerrin McCadden has been a high school English teacher for 3 years and is currently the Chair of her Humanities Department. She is in-

volved in the reconstruction of the humanities curriculum to provide for gender fairness.

- Nancy Cornell has served as a curriculum coordinator in two different school districts over the past 7 years after having been a high school English teacher for 4 years. She also has been a graduate teaching fellow at the University of Vermont.
- Linda Pearo is a middle level teacher on an interdisciplinary team. She works with her students to establish democratic practices and principles in her classroom.

We scheduled a number of meetings, not an easy task in light of the extraordinary demands on these educators' time. The first meeting would be devoted to personal narratives, stories that might get to the heart of what brought these educators to their current democratic commitments. Subsequent meetings would center around discussions of the topics raised in the curriculum theory chapters of this book. Attempting to create a sort of dialogical interplay between curriculum theorists and practitioners, the curriculum leaders were asked to respond critically to the curriculum theory topics in light of their own curriculum practice. As noted in Chapter 1, the group sessions were videotaped, and the tapes were sent to the authors of the curriculum theory chapters, who then were asked to consider the responses of the practitioners in a rewrite of the chapters. The practitioners were given the final manuscript and offered the "final say," in terms of offering up critique or feedback. Kerrin McCadden was asked to write a substantive portion of the last chapter, so that the closing words of this text would embody a practitioner viewpoint.

All of the practitioners in this study embodied what we have come to call democratic curriculum leadership. That is, they are all committed to lifelong inquiry growth, they seek a multilayered understanding of curriculum practice, they engage in a sophisticated part/whole deliberative educational practice, and they engage in the continuous critical awareness of the complex negative/positive dialectic of democratic emancipation. One primary assumption of this study process was that the various perspectives presented in the curriculum theory chapters might enrich and expand these inquiry processes. All agreed that they had not begun their careers with this sophisticated, layered understanding of their practice.

Most of them, in fact, began their careers as fairly traditionally trained teachers, who, once they started teaching, experienced tremendous cognitive dissonance between the practices that were expected of them and what they perceived to be the actual needs of children. For example, Sarah tells us this story:

I didn't start as a democratic, student-centered teacher. When I started teaching, we all taught the grammar book. I did it, even though it bothered me. This was juxtaposed for me by what I noticed in my son's preschool. I would go there in the morning, to this rich environment where the children were active and engaged. Then in the afternoon, I would be confronted with the blank, apathetic faces of the middle schoolers. And I began to ask, what would be the best environment for 12–13-year-olds?

This questioning of the "status quo" led these particular educators to take some risks, in many cases to engage in what they named "subversive" teaching practices. Carol Spencer talks about her early experiences as a Spanish teacher, when she first realized:

The formal curriculum might actually be an impediment to learning. I quickly realized that in this large class of students, about half of them "got it," that is, could learn Spanish in the traditional way, from the grammar book, and half of them didn't "get it." So, I quickly divided the class up into two sections, and half of them learned Spanish the traditional way, with formal grammar instruction, and the other half, well we played games, had conversations . . . and there was only one mandate: that was, when the principal knocked on the door, we had to put away what we were doing, and act like we were "having class."

All of these educators encountered hostility when they sought to do things differently. Jude, for example, was not appreciated by all of the members in the community when she tried to make the gifted and talented curriculum available to a broader range of students. Carol Smith, who has pioneered the development of a student-generated curriculum process in her school, also talked about the resistance she encountered:

There is strife in being innovative—there are times when I have walked into the teacher's room and the conversation stopped. I get paid a lot of money outside my school, outside the state, for consulting. I have yet to be asked for advice by anyone in my school. That's a hard thing.

All of them felt isolated at times—"I couldn't find anyone to talk to"—and all found other "rebels with a cause" through networking with like-minded teachers. This happened for many of them through the middle grades initiative that began a few years ago in Vermont.

Many of the practitioners in the group spoke of never having been exposed to curriculum theory in teacher education courses. They mostly "found their theory" when the need arose because of the cognitive dissonance they experienced in their teaching situations. In the networks that they established, they shared readings and discussed the implications of the ideas. The orientation of their study was eminently practical.

Carol Smith, one of the practicing teachers in the group, expressed little patience with theory that did not find immediate application in her classroom:

> My thing about theory, even today, is I read it, whether it's a book or article or somebody's handout or something about leadership, and if I can't take it home and sleep on it overnight or for a couple of days and bring it into my room and turn it into something, right then, it's gone. If you can't use it and turn it into practice, then there's no point to it at all. If it's about learning and about kids and you can't just say okay and digest it and figure out how to put it into what you do, then it's just not important to me.

This curriculum leader did agree with another group member, however, who suggested that she might find later relevance in something that didn't resonate at the present time. Carol conceded, agreeing that she "changes over time . . . sometimes things haven't 'hatched' yet and I'm just not ready for it. It's about what you're ready to hear."

The willingness to take risks is, for all of these practitioners, intimately connected with a profound concern for students and their learning. Carol Spencer expresses her passion this way: "Transformative leadership in curriculum can't be divorced from a strong belief . . . an incredible belief . . . a driven belief . . . that every kid can get there. Although a lot of people believe it, and say it, it's not enough unless you mean *every kid*." This commitment to the success of all learners and the concomitant diversification of curriculum and instructional practices is a central political issue in Vermont right now, and unfortunately there is something of a backlash against the effort. As one of the group notes: "Elites want their kids to succeed. If other people are able to be smart, the traditional achiever is not necessarily smarter. It's the politics of exclusion—and this is what drives uniformity in schooling."

All of the people in the group agree that the new curriculum framework is a powerful tool for democratic initiatives in education. In fact, says one of them, "it is almost a statement of democratic education." Much of the support for a more democratic education is found in the "Learning Opportunities" section of the *Framework*, which covers such issues as access to resources, both human and material; adaptive learning environments that are tailored to individual student needs; expectations that students will have opportunities to apply their knowledge in meaningful contexts; the use of multiple assessment strategies (including student self-assessment) and the use of assessment to guide student learning; and a curriculum that is interdisciplinary, based on real-life problems, and concerned with personal, community, and global relevance. There is a consensus among these leaders that the document supports a much more innovative approach to education and "forces teachers to become more reflective about their practice." They note that the level of discussion is much richer than ever before, as educators begin to ask the really significant questions about student learning. They also appreciate the fact that learning is no longer just about what children know, and can show on tests and quizzes, but about what children actually can *do*. Applied knowledge, demonstrated through products and performances, is valued.

One of the most important functions of the *Framework*, according to these practitioners, is to serve as a "bridge." People from very different philosophies are now "sitting around the same table" talking about student learning. The *Framework* is designed so that teachers can engage in curriculum design and development from a number of different starting points: They can start from student interests, questions, and concerns; they can start with existing units of study; or they can start with the standards. No one has to throw away what they already do. It thus seems that the *Framework* has, in one sense, provided the "center" around which democratic curriculum deliberations can take place. Despite this rosy assessment, there are a number of problems right now for curriculum leaders. As one practitioner notes:

> There's a lot of political conflict. There's a problem of uninvented school structures that could support children's learning. And there's a high need for accountability. There's a high level of ambiguity in a school system, and that level of ambiguity—that pathway, that chaos, that confusion—is not just a transition to a transformation. It *is* the transformation. We've finally given up the notion that curriculum is external to the learning process. Once the constructivists put their foot in the water, and Gardner put his foot in the water, it was all over. The walls were down. And now that chaos is enormously frightening to parents and confusing to people who don't have kids in school. . . . All the nice little traditional structures that a school principal knows how to play out really have very little to do with believing what Dewey wrote about every kid and the possibility for every kid to learn if we could just create the right school

for them. . . . We need to put our money where our mouth is. If you mean every kid can learn, then very little of the current system can survive, including the old models of orderliness in curriculum.

In summary, the Vermont study group shared a number of experiences and characteristics that contributed to members' growth and development as democratic curriculum leaders. First, they all experienced some initial cognitive dissonance early in their careers when their intuitions and instincts about good teaching came into conflict with bureaucratic expectations. Second, they resolved these contradictions by being willing to take risks and suffer the consequences. Third, they overcame some isolation and occasional hostility to their innovative ideas by seeking out like-minded educators for peer-initiated professional development and continuing study (often, it might be noted, by collective reading and discussion of the ideas of theorists). Fourth, they share an eminently practical relationship to theory. Fifth, they all hold "the learner" central in their curriculum deliberations. And last, they all seem relatively comfortable with the postmodern possibility that democratic curriculum leadership is, at its heart, uncertain, unpredictable, ambiguous, and transformative. They recognize that this type of curriculum leadership challenges the status quo—that is, the taken-for-granted assumptions about the very aims and purposes of public schooling in a society with democratic ideals. It is at its heart a visionary role, for one must be able to point to a future of open-ended possibilities, horizons of human potential as yet unrealized, and the promise of a more democratic society, while at the same time attending to the complex and innumerable details of the day-to-day life in schools. It is no small challenge. And now we turn to the critical curriculum study topics that formed the basis of our conversations about the multifaceted work of democratic curriculum leaders.

REFERENCES

Dewey, J. (1963). *Experience and education.* New York: Collier Books. (Original work published 1938)

Rice, T. W., & Sumberg, A. F. (1997, Winter). Civic culture and government performance in the American states. *Publius: The Journal of Federalism, 27* (1).

Deliberation to Develop School Curricula

GAIL McCUTCHEON

CURRICULUM DEVELOPMENT CONSISTS of activities to address a perplexing set of questions about what should be taught, how that content should be organized, which materials to make available to teachers and students, and other issues related to the content of schooling. It frequently concerns developing a policy for a school or school system about goals for each grade level for a discipline or subject matter (such as one in response to a new set of state standards or a new state model) along with a mission statement and a general philosophy. In my view, many of these sorts of curriculum problems must be resolved at a local level because generalizations about them are unlikely due to differences from one setting to another, such as differences in personnel—students, faculty, administrators—as well as resources, initiatives, expectations, culture, values, school climate, and mission interpretations.

Moreover, developing the curriculum leads to greater understanding of it than when it is done elsewhere and handed on for teachers to use. As a result of local teachers' and administrators' involvement in curriculum development, then, they learn the curriculum intimately as they develop it and can redevelop it in their own classrooms and schools in a valid manner. This occurs because, through teachers' closely examining the curriculum being developed or curriculum materials under consideration, they come to understand more deeply the content they are going to teach.

Hence, it is a natural by-product of the process of curriculum development for those involved in it to understand it more fully, and they

Understanding Democratic Curriculum Leadership. Copyright © 1999 by Teachers College, Columbia University. All rights reserved. ISBN 0-8077-3826-3 (pbk), ISBN 0-8077-3827-1 (cloth). Prior to photocopying items for classroom use, please contact the Copyright Clearance Center, Customer Service, 222 Rosewood Dr., Danvers, MA 01923, USA, tel. (508) 750-8400.

probably come to embrace it even more fully than if they had not been involved because they know the various lines of argument involved at each step and the resolution of conflicts that emerged, so they also can acquire a sense of trust and commitment to the project and what was developed. I think the involvement in curriculum development also leads to a heightened sense of professionalism, as educators realize they are engaging in one of the "Great Conversations" about education—that of what to teach in our schools. So, strong benefits can accompany local curriculum development.

CURRICULUM DELIBERATION

In curriculum work, questions are particularly perplexing; they must be addressed, because some action is needed, but the grounds on which to base decisions are uncertain. Because curriculum problems are practical problems, *deliberation* is a suitable process for treating them (Reid, 1978).

Deliberation is not an esoteric model curriculum theorists designed for curriculum development; deliberation is a practical way in which people solve problems. We deliberate in our everyday lives as we resolve problems with no clear answers, such as how to start preparing for retirement, what to plant on the small hill near the driveway, what meals to plan for the week. Deciding what meals to plan for the week, for instance, means considering nutrition, our family budget, the week's probable time schedule, our family's eating preferences, food preparation, and food storage. A deliberative approach is a decision-making process where people conceive of the problem, create and weigh likely alternative solutions to it, envision probable results of each alternative, and select or develop an optimum course of action. While this definition makes deliberation sound linear, it is not always so, in that while considering matters, deliberators may find it necessary to reframe the original problem they wish to resolve.

My research (McCutcheon, 1995) depicts deliberation occurring both alone—solo deliberation—and in groups. In this chapter, I discuss several fundamental characteristics of deliberation. Further, I provide examples of these in the context of specific curriculum decisions so that readers can envision it more clearly. I also explore several potential implications for curriculum leaders. More details about the nature of deliberation, its fundamental characteristics, and eight case studies of solo and group deliberation can be located in my book (McCutcheon, 1995). My main point is that since most people already deliberate about practical matters in many aspects of their lives, this "natural process" can be applied to local curriculum development. People might need to be reminded of it, but because it is not an artificial process, they do not need extensive training in its methods.

Ideas contributing to deliberation have quite a history. Some are actually traceable to Aristotle's work. Aristotle saw many practical sciences as being interdependent and viewed education as part of politics and as a practical rather than a theoretical or speculative science. Politics, for Aristotle, cannot be an exact science because the "rightness" of actions forming the subject of politics relies extensively on fluctuations in underlying conditions. Aristotle's contributions include his identifying education as a practical science and bringing together moral knowledge and action.

Later, Dewey (1922) termed one kind of thinking "deliberation," characterizing it as a form of practical reasoning that does not separate means from ends or moral from empirical knowledge, somewhat reminiscent of Aristotle's work. Dewey (1922) saw deliberation as a "dramatic rehearsal [in imagination] of various potential lines of action whereby the deliberator envisions a potential action to see what it would entail" (p. 189). Schwab (1978), heavily influenced by Dewey's work, argues that such a method to solve practical problems would be neither deductive nor inductive, but rather deliberative: to choose not the *right* alternative, for there is no such thing, but the *best* one. Reid (1978) continues developing the idea of deliberation as a form of practical reasoning when he characterizes it as "the method by which most everyday practical problems get solved" (p. 43). Walker (1990) also views deliberation as practical reasoning. He thinks practical problems arise when someone points out conditions in need of change. He believes such practical problems can be resolved only by action or a decision to eliminate those problematic conditions. He considers deliberation to be careful consideration of possible actions and the best available knowledge of action likely to be best for the situation.

Roby (1985) delineates several important impediments to deliberation. Two of these occur as deliberators conceptualize the problem. One concerns their *externalizing* elements of the problem when they are not inclined to see themselves as part of the problem. For instance, rather than wondering if they need to change their teaching practices, they simply might blame changes in family patterns and students for difficulties in their practice and achievement test scores. Instead of questioning their own beliefs, biases, habits, assumptions, or other internal factors that might be a part of the problem, these people blame factors external to themselves. One problem with this, aside from the matter that the problem really may be one internal to the people themselves, is that addressing the external factors of the "problem" may not be possible. Teachers can change their own practices within their classrooms, but they have little short-term control over society at large—the socioeconomic nature of their students' families, state policies, and the like. (For a discussion of how teachers can work with others to effect long-term societal and policy changes, see Chapter 5.)

According to Roby (1985), deliberators also impede their initial identification of the "problem" when they *exclude or downplay the curricular commonplaces*. (I will say more about this particular limitation below.) He also notes that a *linear expectation* (the prospect of following some step-by-step procedure) and an *intolerance of uncertainty* can severely limit the entire deliberative process. He further identifies two habits that can negatively impact deliberation. One of these is a *rush to the solution*. An example here is to move to a "pet" solution, whereby deliberators do not question their vested interests or assumptions, but embrace a solution almost blindly. The second habit is a *global mentality*, whereby some universal, and most likely faddish, prescription (e.g., outcome-based education) is held to be a panacea.

Two additional habits can inhibit both problem formulation and reaching optimum resolution, in Roby's view, and these are "either/or thinking" and a "Lone Ranger approach." *Either/or thinking* prevents deliberators from considering alternatives and nuances between two extremes of a continuum, while a *Lone Ranger approach* results in a limited consideration of viable options before acting—individuals act without carefully listening to differing perspectives.

These impediments are important for curriculum leaders to bear in mind while engaging in deliberation so they can alert the group and avert potentially faulty thinking, thereby enabling the group to reach an optimum resolution.

FUNDAMENTAL CHARACTERISTICS OF DELIBERATION

Deliberation, then, consists of a process of socially constructing knowledge about the curriculum to resolve a practical problem. Unraveling this definition and examining some cases of deliberation will make it possible to draw several important features. One of these concerns generating several alternatives, examining them closely, and weighing them and their potential results. Generating alternatives is important because having many alternatives permits deliberators to select or develop the optimum one for their circumstances. Comparing them helps deliberators see the better choices. Perhaps more important, it permits them to understand their own philosophies and theories about each choice and more generally about the content being developed.

Second, productive differences of opinion about alternatives—that is, conflict—are very beneficial in virtually forcing deliberators to examine the alternatives closely. Hence, conflict is to be cherished, not avoided, as long as it can be productive. Thwarting the conflict can be deleterious to the process because full examination of the alternatives would be curtailed or severely diminished. In other words, conflict is the engine driving deliberations, and alternatives are the fuel.

Closely related to the concept of conflict are interests. By this I mean vested interests. A primary contributor to conflict is interest because each deliberator has a vested interest in arguing for a particular position and alternative. For some, this argument is based on the vested interest of already enacting the proposed alternative to some degree, so that it would be easier if that curriculum policy were enacted than another because less change would be involved. For others, the proposed alternative may be in accord with their own theory of child development, the nature of knowledge, or other matters, so it would be in their interest to see that alternative adopted. When people's vested interests differ, conflict can ensue, but, as I have pointed out, conflict is highly important in causing deliberators to examine each alternative meticulously.

Several excerpts from a case study on curriculum deliberation (McCutcheon, 1995) illustrate these three characteristics very well and also demonstrate their interrelationships. In this case, several teachers representing different schools, led by an administrator, are deciding which reading textbooks to recommend for purposes of adoption. By agreement with the teachers' professional association, teachers vote on the final decision as to which textbook is to be adopted. But first, a group nominates which books to place on the ballot for teachers at large to consider.

Several deliberators are in this group. Among them is Robin, who teaches at a school where teachers are developing a philosophy and approach based on open education and a whole language approach to teaching language arts. In Robin's view,

"Students learn how to be at home in their language by using it. We shouldn't artificially separate reading from writing, spelling, grammar, and so forth. They should all be integrated because when kids talk, they're also learning something about listening, reading, and writing, and vice versa. These are all communication skills, so they are the language arts. We shouldn't teach word-attack skills because English goes against phonics rules more often than it follows them. Students learn how to read by reading a lot. That way kids generate their own rules about reading, not by memorizing and applying someone else's rules on worksheets and then applying them when they're reading stories and novels." (McCutcheon, 1995, p. 161)

Clearly, it would be in Robin's interest to adopt a series of books in line with this practical theory because it would take less effort to adapt the materials to this set of beliefs. By contrast, Audey believes that children learn how to read "by applying different word-attack skills to unfamiliar words, so children need to have a healthy dose of phonics, context clues, rhyming-word families" (p. 166). Just as it would be in Robin's interest to adopt materials in line with her practical theory, so would it be in Audey's best interest to adopt materials in line with her, markedly different, practical theory. Also in this group is Lauren, who believes that "children need exciting stories and factual articles to read. Kids here have very low language ability. I think it's because of their homes. I bet they rarely get to talk much at home. They don't go to the public library. We need good things for them to read and discuss so they will read them and practice language use" (p. 161).

Today's meeting is near the end of the deliberations. The group begins by examining the materials under consideration, displayed on various tables around the room. When the meeting is called to order, Robin states, "You know, I really think we need materials to use to reintegrate the language arts. When we teach them in an integrated way, the various skills support each other. I like Holt." Audey wonders aloud whether "teachers would accept the kind of testing included with the Holt materials, though. It seems so subjective. Can most of the teachers do this? Would the administration make us write a test?" The administrator in charge of overseeing the textbook adoption reminds teachers of the state law applicable to this question, saying, "You must test the pupil performance objectives in our graded course of study," and then quotes from the Holt teacher's guide about the philosophy on evaluating students' progress. Audey grumbles softly, but audibly, "We aren't ready for that here in Mapleton." Robin claims a willingness to go to anyone in the school district and argue that by using Holt's program all the pupil performance objectives can be covered: "I'd love to go to the school board to explain this." Lauren remarks, "It's a political choice," without elaboration. Robin disagrees: "We have to choose the best program, not just make a decision we know the board will approve." Lauren claims this is idealistic, but Robin shakes her head vehemently in disagreement.

The administrator in charge of the selection process says, "Holt really scares me to death. It's so different. But this is a democratic process. I just worry that we're not ready for it here in Mapleton. Remember, you're representing the 90% of teachers who aren't here." Lauren adds, "One poem [in Holt] really bothers me. I don't like their selection." Another deliberator remarks, "The trade books with the Heath program . . . they're contrived trade books. And do we get class sets? Five copies? One? What do we do with them?" Robin agrees: "Yes, that's crucial. I think it's pretty clear they're the future for teaching reading." The administrative leader puts a halt to the discussion by saying, "Okay, we're ready to vote now," and gives the group directions about how to vote for the best series to place on the ballot.

This excerpt is interesting in demonstrating the relationship between conflict and interest and its potential for forcing people to examine alternatives closely. Robin's belief in whole language led her to present those views to the group, as Audey's views made her skeptical of the program Robin favored. I think a leader who understood deliberation better might have led this group to examine more closely what each set of materials had to offer in terms of its theory of reading and the consequent strengths and weaknesses of materials they offered. Instead of forcing a vote, the deliberators might well have reached a decision out of their deliberations by developing a socially constructed view about which materials were best for Mapleton. Several flaws were apparent in this process. For one, the group was far too large for genuine deliberations to develop well. Because of the teachers' association agreement with the administration about the process, representation was needed from each school, bringing the size to more than 30 and rendering face-to-face deliberations all but impossible as teachers sat around the periphery of a huge, barn-like room. Further, it was unfortunate that the administrator took a position about her dislike of the Holt materials; if the decision about what to recommend had been truly in the hands of the teachers, this would not have occurred. The administrator's view affected the group's decision. Although the Holt materials did place second in the teacher's voting, a different set of materials was ultimately adopted by the group.

While the triad of examining alternatives closely, conflict, and interest are probably the most crucial characteristics of deliberation and are highly interrelated, others also are important. For one, deliberation has a moral nature in that it is not a totally objective, value-free enterprise, nor should it be. Decisions about the curriculum are inescapably informed by values, ethical commitments, a sense of social responsibility, and a vision of a better society.

Deliberation also has a social nature, and perhaps the most important dimension here is the fact that the group socially constructs knowledge through the natural give-and-take of the discussion about the curriculum issue being considered. For this reason, had the group in the excerpt above been smaller and allowed to continue its discussion, it probably would have arrived at a socially constructed decision about which materials to recommend. A vote would not have been needed. To be fair, the administrator was under the press of time because it was near the end of the school year, and she needed a decision to permit the vote of the entire teaching faculty so materials could be ordered in time for the beginning of the following school year. In addition, deliberation is a social enterprise because the concept of the "good" democratic society informs collaborative decisions and thus provides an ethical context for all decisions. (Chapter 1 provides an overview of this ethical context.) Additionally, because educators share the responsibility for educating children and youth well, it is a social enterprise. Moreover, deliberators need to apply social skills in exchanging ideas and in creating a consensus over what they are developing and what their final decisions will be.

Several characteristics can be gleaned from Schwab's (1978) work. Schwab uses the term "commonplaces" to refer to several areas of focus helpful in organizing the uncertainty and variability of curriculum problems. The commonplaces constitute another set of fundamental characteristics of deliberation, for I find they are themes underlying the deliberative work in many groups. Schwab urges us to apply four bodies of knowledge to curriculum problems. These are knowledge of subject matter, learners, milieus, and teachers. His fifth body of knowledge concerns the crucial work of the curriculum specialist who is to monitor the proceedings of the group and point out to the group what has occurred, what is currently occurring, and what has yet to be considered. Schwab urges continuous reflection when considering the commonplaces and their application to specific curriculum problems, and he wants the curriculum specialist to be very thoughtful about how best to facilitate the group's decisions. However, Schwab (1978) depicts deliberation more formally than I do, although Dewey (1922) argues that deliberation is a form of thinking.

A "final" characteristic of deliberation to be discussed here is simultaneity, the idea that many matters simultaneously vie for attention and sometimes are treated almost at the same time. One example here is of a group trying to develop a curriculum that would be sufficiently challenging, yet doable, for the students in a school system. The group might suggest one idea for consideration, then almost immediately correct itself because the idea fell short on one dimension of their criteria for a good curriculum—for example, it might be sufficiently challenging, but not practical because it was too advanced for the students.

SOLO AND GROUP DELIBERATION

Both solo and group deliberation bear these characteristics. Solo deliberation, as the term implies, happens alone as teachers plan lessons preactively (before teaching) and interactively (while teaching), then reflect on teaching (postactive planning) after the action, which informs future preactive and interactive planning. When teachers plan lessons at a highly detailed level, less interactive planning occurs. This seems to be more the case for novice teachers than for highly experienced ones. Perhaps it is because novice teachers, in an effort to deal with their own insecurity, preplan to a great extent. At any rate, preplanning in great detail seems to create conditions in which teachers focus more on the content and less on students and what is unfolding in the lesson. When teachers preactively plan lessons more broadly, they alter the original idea and elaborate on it in the process of teaching.

Teachers' plans generally follow their own theories of action—their interrelated beliefs about what students should learn, how they learn, how the class is best structured and organized for learning to occur, classroom discipline, and other important matters of practice. Many teachers develop routines within which they improvise, such as arranging for learning centers to treat particular skills or parts of the curriculum, and assigning students to these centers through a checkoff system. My own research shows that teachers plan in accordance with their theories of action. Indeed, no teacher's actions contradicted those theories.

Obviously, the chief difference between solo and group deliberation is that during group deliberation more voices and ideas are present, so true generation and examination of alternatives can occur because of conflict. However, even in solo deliberation teachers conceive of alternatives, and conflict can occur when they are "of two minds" about a decision. As is true of group deliberation, having alternatives permits close examination of the benefits and shortcomings of each.

SOME IMPLICATIONS FOR DEMOCRATIC CURRICULUM LEADERS

I am not arrogant enough to consider writing about every implication of the deliberative ideal in this section, but I want to raise and discuss several I believe are important. Given this description of deliberation, what implications can be drawn for democratic curriculum leaders to increase the likelihood of the group making optimum decisions?

One concerns the nature of the process itself. Describing deliberation as a process of conceiving of the problem, generating alternatives, examining them closely through the process of a social construction of reality fueled by conflict and interest about the alternatives, and selecting among the alternatives or creating the best one, makes the process sound linear, but it is not always so. This is because as people generate and consider alternatives, they may find it necessary to go back and reshape the original problem or perhaps examine some previously tacit assumptions they held about goals and the nature of the education they are trying to develop, assumptions about their attributions of students and other teachers in the schools, and the like.

Because it is not linear, because several alternatives are considered, and because multiple perspectives cause conflict, deliberation frequently seems grossly inefficient and always takes a great deal of time. This often results in a press of time as a deadline nears, which easily can lead to stress. Stress may be the most significant difficulty in deliberation, for the very effects of stress directly oppose important characteristics of deliberation. Research has shown that the effects of stress include cognitive oversimplification, the narrowing of perspective, disregarding of alternatives, disorganization, forgetfulness, and impatience (McCutcheon, 1995). Each of these obviously can have devastating influences on the deliberative process; stress significantly affects the thinking and deliberative potential by bringing about a rush to complete the task in order to remove the stressor. This seems to have been the case in the excerpt above, where decisions were oversimplified and alternatives were not considered carefully.

The Holt materials were criticized on several counts, but other materials were not examined carefully for their strengths and weaknesses and their fit (or lack of fit) with Mapleton's teachers. It may be helpful for leaders to stay organized and to point out to the group what their accomplishments have been. In an effort to dispel some of the stress and its influences, one Ohio curriculum leader also plans some social occasions near the end of the process—such as a quick lunch—where deliberations are not to be discussed. Time is clearly an important factor here, and it is important to anticipate sufficient time to complete the project so a realistic deadline is established.

Second, generating alternatives is a crucial dimension of this process because having several possibilities forces the group to examine each closely rather than adopting the first acceptable idea that comes along. It may be important for the leader to introduce several ideas so that alternatives are present in the deliberations. For example, one Ohio curriculum leader routinely brings to the group suggestions of learned societies (such as the National Council of Social Studies) or scholars, or examples of curricula from other forward-thinking school systems so deliberators can see several alternative ways of thinking about the task and possible resolutions of it. Further, he acknowledges the existence of conflict and its beneficial nature, but keeps encouraging deliberators to think about what is needed for their community, perhaps in an effort to help them rise above their vested interests to seek the common good (McCutcheon, 1995).

Third, because the process rests on a *social* construction of knowledge, group composition and size are important considerations. People holding different theories of action would be helpful to support conflict. Further, group size needs to be sufficiently small to permit the ready exchange of ideas and elaboration on them in a face-to-face manner. When an entire group must be larger than this for an unavoidable reason, it might be helpful to break into subgroups to examine particular matters in great detail.

Just as interests affect group deliberation, teachers' personal theories of action influence solo deliberation. This is one reason why when one group develops the curriculum, then passes it to another to teach it, the curriculum being taught is not always what the developers had in mind. Yet, by the same token, many teachers develop astoundingly creative and worthwhile practices. In many schools this problem of teachers' not following the curriculum is treated by having a supervisor check that teachers are following the curriculum, but there may be a more professional, educative way to treat this. Some of the materials and practices teachers create are probably adoptable by other teachers, so it seems that it would be helpful if teachers were to create small deliberative bodies in schools, at grade levels, in departments, or in teams, to talk about their practices, trade ideas that work well for them, share or create materials, observe one another to see each other's practices, and the like.

Seeing the problem of what to teach, and what to use to teach it, as a group endeavor might be helpful in resolving the issue and could lead to more careful consideration than is possible through solo deliberation. This is because in the group varying theories of action might cause conflict. People in the group would understand their endeavors better, and a collegial sense of ownership of the curriculum at the school or grade level or within the department or team could develop, perhaps motivating some to become more involved in their teaching. This could be beneficial also in creating conditions for a form of professional development to occur at a very local level.

SPECIFIC ADVICE

In the context of this general discussion of democratic curriculum deliberation, several specific tips can be offered on how to provide leadership for this very collaborative process.

Careful planning. The first set of matters here concerns planning before the group begins its work. One matter to consider is the composition of the deliberative group. Clearly, its size should be sufficiently small so eye contact can be established and maintained among group members. Second, members need to hold varying views and have different expertise to promote the generation of alternatives and to enhance conflict, which virtually will force people to examine those alternatives closely. Representation of people who know a great deal about the content, about the students, about the teachers, and about the context also seems in order, as Schwab (1978) has suggested.

Appropriate setting. In addition to determining group membership, another matter important to consider in planning is the setting or location for meetings. Remembering the importance of eye contact for the participants to become a genuine group, a room with a large table might be helpful. Other, smaller areas for subgroups to work in are also useful. One central Ohio curriculum leader begins the work each day in a room with a large table, breaks the groups into subgroups in adjacent rooms as needed, then has the group return to the large-table room to summarize its accomplishments and discuss them before breaking for the day.

Sufficient time. A third matter to remember in planning for the deliberations is the importance of allowing sufficient time. Not only does a curriculum need to be developed, but so does the group. While this occurs simultaneously, it is rarely quick and efficient, and it cannot be rushed. For this reason, some social time, such as coffee breaks, should be fit into the schedule.

Inclusive practices. Just as the nature of the deliberative process has implications for planning effective strategies, it also has implications for the democratic leadership of the actual process. One clear implication is that the leader should begin meetings in an inclusive manner to facilitate the social construction of meaning. For example, one skilled curriculum leader in central Ohio opens the first meeting by introducing group members in a clever way. He brags to the group about particular accomplishments of each group member, almost to the point of embarrassing the group members. For instance, in a recent initial meeting to redevelop the social studies curriculum, he was heard to say:

> Paula here was involved with "Project Business"; Kent teaches some fascinating courses about the Orient, and James uses some magnificent simulations about the Constitution and Arab–Israeli conflict. Sheila and Laurel from Hastings [Elementary School] are exploring the history of our town in splendid detail through speakers, field trips, and readings. (McCutcheon, 1995, p. 178)

These introductions and flattering comments may have helped people see each other's expertise and commitment to social studies education by setting a tone of respect for their accomplishments. Planning informal time to socialize is also important throughout the process.

Task orientation. It is important to consider how to introduce the task and to do so in a manner that is clear yet open enough to be reformulated somewhat if that is appropriate. This is because what might have been considered to be the curriculum problem might not be the problem in need of attention, for it might be nested in a larger curriculum problem that must be addressed in order to repair the smaller one. It is also true that the group may offer different views on the nature of what needs to be done, given the curriculum problem.

Active facilitation. During sessions, it is important for the leader to be an active participant and leader by listening closely and engaging in deliberations. While the leader should not take a side (as was the case in the textbook adoption example cited above), it is important to help people clarify ideas and to lead the group in summarizing its accomplishments. Summing up can be beneficial to groups by helping them become aware of what they have accomplished, decisions to date, and what remains to be done. It is obviously important also to serve the enterprise by providing secretarial support and amenities such as beverages and snacks for breaks.

DEMOCRATIC PROFESSIONAL GROWTH

Just as many other professionals learn about their practice through reflecting on it as they employ a new strategy, so can curriculum leaders. Curriculum leaders are well advised to use solo deliberation about conceiving of and employing democratic principles instead of controlling curriculum development. Here, curriculum leaders would consider various ways to proceed and judge them using as a criterion whether a particular strategy would be likely to nurture the group's deliberation rather than whether it merely would get the job done most efficiently. I am arguing here for curriculum leaders to attend to their own professional development by actively focusing on it reflectively.

This might be enhanced through group reflection on the process and on strategies being developed and utilized. Such group reflection could occur either through occasional face-to-face meetings or over e-mail, perhaps through a study chat group of curriculum leaders.

Some leaders also might benefit by maintaining a reflective journal where brief comments could be noted. One advantage of this is that the focus of writing (or word processing) in the journal directs attention to the ideas so they might be developed more fully or reflected upon more deeply than in the absence of the journal. Another advantage of this is the ability to reread ideas. Rereading the journal can help reflective curriculum leaders spot trends and patterns worthy of greater attention.

Further readings about reflective practice also might be in order, although I believe concerted and sustained reflection-in-action and -on-action in facilitating the group's progress and development of both the curriculum and the group itself is likely to be more helpful. This is because such reflection is highly personalized, active learning about one's own practice as a curriculum leader. The problem here is one of how to understand democratic curriculum deliberation in action, not just on a theoretical or philosophical level. And I believe the best way to do this is to reflect on one's actions toward this end, to alter the actions as warranted, and to reflect further in a group or alone, rather than to read further about it.

REFERENCES

Dewey, J. (1922). *Human nature and conduct.* New York: Henry Holt.

McCutcheon, G. (1995). *Developing the curriculum: Solo and group deliberation.* White Plains, NY: Longman.

Reid, W. (1978). *Thinking about the curriculum.* London: Routledge & Kegan Paul.

Roby, T. (1985). Habits impeding deliberation. *Journal of Curriculum Studies, 17*(1), 7–36.

Schwab, J. (1978). *Science, curriculum, and liberal education: Selected essays* (I. Westbury & N. D. Wilkof, Eds.). Chicago: University of Chicago Press.

Walker, D. F. (1990). *Fundamentals of curriculum.* New York: Harcourt Brace Jovanovich.

Understanding Curriculum Systems

NOEL GOUGH

In Oliver Stone's (1995) movie, *Nixon,* there is a scene at the Lincoln Memorial in which Richard Nixon is confronted by a group of antiwar protesters, including a young woman with whom he has a brief conversation:

> Woman: You can't stop it [the Vietnam war], can you? Even if you want to . . . 'cos it's not you, it's the system. The system won't let you stop it.
>
> Nixon: There's . . . uh . . . more at stake here than what you want and what I want.
>
> Woman: Then what's the point? What's the point of being President? You're powerless!
>
> Nixon: No . . . no, I'm not powerless—because . . . because I understand the system. I believe I can . . . er . . . control it—maybe not control it totally but . . . er . . . tame it enough to make it do some good.
>
> Woman: Sounds like you're talking about a wild animal.
>
> Nixon: Yeah—maybe I am.

This brief scene raises many of the questions that we[1] may need to ask if we want to "understand the system" in which we work, whether it is a system of national governance or a smaller organizational structure such as a school or school district. What does it mean to understand an administrative system as something that actually might *prevent* its leaders

Understanding Democratic Curriculum Leadership. Copyright © 1999 by Teachers College, Columbia University. All rights reserved. ISBN 0-8077-3826-3 (pbk), ISBN 0-8077-3827-1 (cloth). Prior to photocopying items for classroom use, please contact the Copyright Clearance Center, Customer Service, 222 Rosewood Dr., Danvers, MA 01923, USA, tel. (508) 750-8400.

from taking morally responsible action, and perhaps even render them "powerless"? Is it meaningful to think of a system as some kind of organism—as "a wild animal" that needs to be "tamed" before it can be made to "do some good"? Is a bureaucratic system a material reality or is it, to borrow William Gibson's (1984) description of cyberspace, a "consensual hallucination" (p. 12) that exists chiefly because most of us behave *as if* it existed? How have we come to think of organizations such as schools, school districts, and other educational bureaucracies as systems? What kinds of systems do we imagine them to be, and what is "systematic" about them?

As has already been stated, the overall purpose of this book is to help democratic curriculum leaders cultivate a *deep understanding* of their practice.[2] My specific purpose in this chapter is to suggest some ways in which such a deep understanding might be cultivated with respect to educational systems. My starting point is to suggest that one way of deepening our understanding of the systems in which we work is, quite literally, to do some digging—to emulate the archaeologist's method of studying material culture and attempt to excavate the sedimented history of systems thinking.[3] Unearthing the traces of the ways we have made sense of educational systems in the past (and the tools with which they were made) not only helps us to recognize their continuing affinities with current ways of thinking, but also may help us to anticipate or generate alternative ways of "systematizing" education in the future.

This chapter is organized in four main parts. First, I consider briefly the materials from which systems are constructed so that, like an archaeologist, we have some idea of what we are looking for when we start digging. Second, I consider some of the implications for current administrative practices of what I have exposed in the course of my own digging. In the third section, I critically examine claims that chaos and complexity theories may provide new and improved ways of thinking about curriculum administration systems. In the fourth section, I advance an argument that I presently find most persuasive, namely, that narrative theory—curriculum as storytelling—provides us with many critical and creative conceptual tools for both understanding and improving the practice of curriculum leadership. I conclude with a very brief review of the key strategic ideas for democratic curriculum leadership introduced in this chapter.

THE MATERIAL ARTIFACTS OF CURRICULUM

Like school teaching (and many other aspects of cultural life), the conceptual history of curriculum leadership is manifested in material artifacts. Most of these are either texts (print documents, overhead projector transparencies, audiotapes, videotapes, and computer disks) or the inscription devices that are used for producing and reading them. Until quite recently, a curriculum historian's primary sources were "fossilized" words on paper—if a curriculum document goes through several drafts, it is at least possible that each could be archived—whereas now much of the work that curriculum developers do is recorded in electronic traces that can be modified or erased with a single keystroke.

A critical issue for curriculum leaders at this time concerns the appropriateness of continuing to produce, reproduce, and privilege the dominant artifact of curriculum administration—the print-on-paper curriculum document—in the light of the textual alternatives that are now available. For example, the educational bureaucracies of the states of Vermont (in the United States) and Victoria (in Australia), recently have produced print documents that clearly are intended, in each case, to function as instruments for organizing the curriculum work undertaken within their respective jurisdictions. Although I have heard curriculum leaders in Vermont testify to the "flexibility" and "adaptability" of *Vermont's Framework of Standards and Learning Opportunities* (Vermont, State Board of Education, 1996a), it initially was disseminated in the relatively inflexible medium of print—or what is tellingly called "hard" copy. During 1997, more than a year after its print publication, the *Framework* was published electronically on the Vermont Board of Education's website, although the accompanying document, *Core Connections: A How-to Guide for Using Vermont's Framework* (Vermont, State Board of Education, 1996b), still has not been made available in that form. However, the state of Victoria's 8-volume *Curriculum and Standards Framework* (Victoria, Board of Studies, 1995) was disseminated simultaneously in print and on computer disks, with much of the accompanying advice on implementation published on interactive, searchable CD-ROMs and websites. These electronic forms implicitly invite users to edit and adapt the text, and this is precisely what I have observed many school-based teams of curriculum workers doing. I must emphasize that I am *not* suggesting that the electronic publication of the *Curriculum and Standards Framework* necessarily implies that Victoria's Board of Studies is any more democratic or liberatory in its intentions than Vermont's Board of Education.[4] Rather, I am suggesting that democratic curriculum leaders might be well advised to heed Foucault's (1969/1972) warning that "in our time, history is that which transforms *documents* into *monuments*" (p. 7; emphasis in original), and actively seek to have curriculum policies and advice disseminated in media that are monumentalized less easily than are printed texts.

But the significance of the new electronic media technologies for curriculum leadership is likely to go far beyond the provision of curriculum information on disk or via the Internet. The digital convergence of broadcasting, publishing, and computing within new global circuits of information and virtualization also might suggest more appropriate and generative models for curriculum work than have been provided previously. One long-standing tradition of curriculum administration (which I will describe in more detail in the next section) has represented curriculum as a *closed system* of discrete components (objectives, content, process, products) interacting in linear cause-and-effect relationships. Furthermore, many of these components, and the "spaces" they occupy, have been conceptualized as material objects. For example, the term "content" suggests that a curriculum is like a *container* (an object with bounded spatial dimensions), while references to "frameworks," "standards," and the flow-charts used to depict planning sequences invoke the technical languages of manufacturing industries.

However, during the past 2 decades, a number of influential curriculum scholars have been using a less mechanistic language. For example, Grumet (1981) describes curriculum as "the collective story we tell our children about our past, our present, and our future" (p. 115). In some respects, this *narrative turn* (to which I will return in the final section of this chapter) can be understood as a deliberate dematerialization of curriculum-as-object into curriculum-as-text. Twenty years ago, the idea of curriculum as a "collective story" could be resisted by bureaucratic curriculum administrators as being too theoretical, too nebulous, too abstract—and, of course, too threatening: how does one "manage" or "control" storytelling? Today, the concept of curriculum-as-story may seem much less esoteric, since our growing familiarity with virtual reality technologies has changed our sense of the relationships between material and informational worlds. If you or your children regularly surf the net, play computer games, or nurture a cyberpet (such as a Tamagotchi), the idea of a virtual world of information that coexists with the material world of objects is definitely *not* an abstraction.

A BRIEF ARCHAEOLOGY OF CURRICULUM SYSTEMS

While the key components of curriculum systems are informational patterns (such as statements of objectives, content, standards, and so on), they invariably have been represented as material objects. The language of curriculum administration is still infused with the residues of attempts to model organizations on industrial systems of producing, transforming, and transporting materials—the so-called "factory" model of schooling. For example, William Doll and Al Alcazar (1998) argue that Frederick Taylor's (1911/1947) paradigm of "scientific management" dominated

American social, industrial, managerial, and organizational thought from the second to (at least) the seventh decades of the twentieth century and remains a force today, although what was overt and explicit in the earlier decades has since become "natural" to our way of thinking. Through his time-and-motion studies of pig iron handlers at the Bethlehem Steel Company in 1896, and by controlling the handlers' actions with stop-watch precision, Taylor (1911/1947, p. 43) increased their productivity by nearly 400%. Doll and Alcazar (1998) argue that Taylor's concept of control (imposed, overt, top-down, centralized) is now buried deep within the American meaning of organization (to the extent that organization and control are almost synonymous) and that, in terms of educational organization, this sense of control has become "the ghost in the curriculum" (p. 295). However, if we excavate a little further and examine how pigs were handled some 70 years prior to Taylor's studies of pig iron handlers, it appears that Taylor merely named a concept of control that is buried even more deeply than Doll and Alcazar suggest. Writing of the mechanization of the U.S. meat industry, Siegfried Giedion (1948) notes that in the 1830s "systematic teamwork was introduced in the killing and dressing of hogs. The assembly-line attitude is present before it can be applied in mechanized form to complicated machine processes" (p. 78). Giedion also observed that, in the abattoirs, "killing itself . . . cannot be mechanized. It is upon organization that the burden falls" (p. 246).

Marshall McLuhan (1951) underlines the necessity for being alert to the ways in which disparate cultural activities may be connected by similar principles of order and control:

> When we see the scientific techniques of mass killing applied with equal indifference in the abattoirs, in the Nazi death camps, and on the battlefields, we can afford to ask whether our habit of bringing death within the orbit of our . . . industrial procedures is altogether sound. In fact, this tendency would seem to play a vivid spotlight on much that is radically unsound in our daily patterns of existence. There is a kind of trancelike dream logic in extending the methods and attitudes of one sphere of action to another. But is it consistent with the purposes of consciousness or even of continued existence? (p. 15)

McLuhan states an extreme case of the dangerous yet persistent tendency in our society to impose rational principles generated in one set of circumstances onto others. I find it no less frightening that a highly influential curriculum scholar like George Beauchamp (1968) could devote a whole chapter of both editions of *Curriculum Theory* to the concept of "curriculum engineering,"[5] a term that he used to represent both "the curriculum system" and "its internal dynamics":

> Curriculum engineering consists of all of the processes necessary to make a curriculum system functional in schools. The chief engineers in the curriculum system are the superintendent of schools, principals, and curriculum directors. . . . They, the engineers, organize and direct the manipulation of the various tasks and operations that must go on in order for a curriculum to be planned, implemented in classrooms through the instructional program, evaluated, and revised in light of the data accumulated through evaluation. Thus, curriculum engineering encompasses the set of activities necessary to keep the curriculum of a school in a dynamic state. (pp. 108–109)

While such a crude mechanism subsequently was opposed by some curriculum theorists,[6] others refined Taylor's principles of scientific management by appropriating the language of the relatively new field of cybernetics—the study of systems in which both humans (and other organisms) and machines are understood in terms of information processing. Thus, for example, Francis Hunkins (1980) asserted that "the cybernetic principle" was "essential to the monitoring aspect of program maintenance":

> Cybernation permits rationalization of the total managerial activities related to maintaining the program. It supplies data requisite for decision-making. Cybernation frees curriculum managers from petty distractions and enables these leaders to make decisions based on substantial data. With cybernation, curriculum decision-makers have much greater latitude in locating their facilities' efficiency, their curriculum elements' effectiveness in relation to initial intentions and current supply of resources. (p. 324)

Hunkins (1980) acknowledges that "some might argue that cybernation is fine when working with machines, but inappropriate when dealing with individuals in schools" (p. 324). Nevertheless, he argues that "the components of a cybernetic system are present in most schools":

> Objectives are usually present; groups of individuals exist for making judgments; resources are available; processes of evaluation are noted. . . . Effective curriculum development creates inputs, devises systems of transforming these inputs into programs, develops procedures for introducing these programs, identifies means for evaluation, and develops avenues for feeding information back into the curriculum system. (pp. 324–325)

Given the recent proliferation of cyberwords—cyborgs, cyberspace, cyberpunks, cybercafes—Hunkins's invocation of cybernation may seem to be unexceptional. Since the term *cybernetics* was coined in the 1940s,[7] the field has developed as an interdisciplinary science in which organisms and machines are all able to be understood in terms of concepts such as feedback loops, signal transmission, and goal-oriented behavior. Unlike Hunkins's straw persons, I see nothing inappropriate about including humans in cybernetic circuits or networks—like Donna Haraway (1991), I am not afraid of my kinship with machines (see also Gough, 1995). But cybernetics is not uncontested conceptual territory and there is more than one "cybernetic principle." The question of *which* cybernetic principles appeal to curriculum administrators still working with the factory model is raised by David Pratt's (1980) application of "a cybernetic perspective" to the problem of "managing aptitude differences":

> The problem of maintaining consistently high achievement from a group of learners who differ in aptitude and other characteristics can be seen as an instance of the general question of how a system with variable input can be designed to produce stable output. Phrased in this way, the question lies squarely within the field of cybernetics, the study of self-regulation in systems. (p. 335)

Pratt (1980) uses the regulation of temperature in a building as an example of a simple cybernetic system, and then uses temperature regulation in the human body to illustrate his assertion that "the most elegant and complex cybernetic systems are found in nature" (p. 335). The unexamined assumption in Pratt's argument is that curriculum systems and cybernetic systems *should* be "designed to produce stable output." By his choice of examples, Pratt seems to assume that some sense of natural order—in this case stable output—should inform curriculum work and that cybernetics can help us to achieve it.

But the concept of homeostasis—the ability of an organism to maintain itself in a stable state—is only one of the key ideas that has informed cybernetics during the past half-century. As Katherine Hayles (1994) points out, during the period from roughly 1945 to 1960, homeostasis provided cybernetics with meanings that were deeply conservative, "privileging constancy over change, predictability over complexity, equilibrium over evolution" (p. 446). However, even in these early years, homeostasis competed with the concept of reflexivity ("turning a system's rules back on itself so as to cause it to engage in more complex behavior" [Hayles, 1994, p. 446]), which led "away from the closed circle of corrective feedback, privileging change over constancy, evolution over equilibrium, complexity over predictability" (p. 446). Hayles (1994) further argues that, in broader social terms, "homeostasis reflected the desire for a 'return to normalcy' after the maelstrom of World War II. By contrast, reflexivity pointed toward the open horizon of an unpredictable and increasingly complex postmodern world" (p. 446).

In Hayles's (1994) brief history of cybernetics, reflexivity displaces homeostasis as a key concept in the period from 1960 to about 1972, after which the emphasis shifts to *emergence*, with interest focused "not on how systems maintain their organization intact, but rather on how they evolve in unpredictable and often highly complex ways through emergent processes" (p. 463). Hayles emphasizes that concepts such as homeostasis and reflexivity do not disappear altogether but linger on in various ways and may exert an inertial weight that limits the ways in which newer concepts may be deployed.

In the case of Hunkins's and Pratt's selective appropriations of cybernetic principles, we might well ask why curriculum theorists in 1980 were still privileging conceptions of homeostatic self-regulation, two decades after they had ceased to be generative in the field of cybernetics itself. I suspect that, unlike cyberneticists, curriculum scholars were faced with few compelling challenges to the deeply sedimented conceptions of "natural" order to which Pratt alludes—order as stability, predictability, and equilibrium.[8]

I believe that most educational bureaucracies are still governed by a systematic rationality that privileges orderly and predictable processes culminating (as Pratt would have it) in "stable output." In these systems, curriculum documents (like Vermont's and Victoria's *Framework* documents) function as homeostatic devices, regulating the diverse inputs of students and teachers by bringing them within closed circuits of corrective feedback in order to maintain stability and equilibrium. Democratic curriculum leaders who concur with this analysis then are faced with questions about their own possibilities for strategic action. How can we act to reflexively disturb the equilibrium of the systems in which we work, to provide opportunities for unpredictable, complex, and unstable outputs to emerge? I will briefly outline here two possible courses of action: One involves an exploration of the possibilities of chaos and complexity theories for curriculum work, while the other involves paying more sustained attention to the implications of understanding curriculum work as interrelated networks of textual production and interpretation.

TURNING TO CHAOS AND COMPLEXITY

One possible conclusion that might be drawn from my archaeology of systematic rationality in curriculum administration is that *if* we are to continue to see curriculum systems in cybernetic terms, then we at least should work with concepts such as reflexivity and emergence, rather than homeostasis, so that our work is oriented toward the complexities of unpredictable change and evolution. This is, in fact, the kind of systems thinking that characterizes the work of a number of curriculum theorists who, over the past decade or so, have sought to reconceptualize curriculum work in terms of chaos and complexity theory. For example, William Doll (1986, 1989, 1993) and Daiyo Sawada and Michael Caley (1985) were among the first curriculum scholars to explore the meaning of chaos for curriculum inquiry and outline some of the theoretical and practical consequences of reconceptualizing curriculum in terms of metaphors generated by chaos theory, drawing particular attention to the evolutionary potential of *disequilibrium*. More recently, Catherine Ennis (1992) has described learning as a dynamical open system, and Eric MacPherson (1995) has asserted that chaos theory represents a "new paradigm," heralding a scientific and cultural revolution with significant implications for reorganizing curricula according to such principles as nonlinearity, irreversibility, and self-organization.

Among these scholars, Doll (1993) has perhaps made the most practical contribution to curriculum leadership by translating chaos theory into four criteria, which can actually be used to guide the generation of a transformative (rather than stable) curriculum. He calls these criteria his "four Rs": richness, recursion, relations, and rigor (p. 176). It is beyond the scope of this chapter to describe these criteria in detail, but Doll's own account of them is very accessible, and highly recommended. To summarize some key features of Doll's four Rs, *richness* "refers to a curriculum's depth, to its layers of meaning, to its multiple possibilities or interpretations" (p. 176); richness is supplied by "disturbing qualities," including *"indeterminacy, anomaly, inefficiency, chaos,* [and] *disequilibrium"* and "provocative generative . . . *problematics, perturbations,* [and] *possibilities"* (p. 176; emphasis in original). These are to be "continually negotiated among students, teachers, and texts" (p. 176) and echo Garth Boomer's (1982) curriculum principle of "connecting": "The more richly the teacher can spin a tapestry of metaphor and analogy into a thick redundant text . . . , the more likely it is that students will find a way in" (p. 120). Doll's (1993) second term, *recursion,* is "associated with the mathematical operation of iteration . . . [in which] a formula is run over and over, with the output of one equation being the input for the next" (p. 177); however, *recursion* in the sense that Doll uses it "refers less to mathematics and more to the human capacity of having thoughts loop back on themselves" (p. 177). As Doll infers from Schwab's work on "the practical" (pp. 162–163), such "recursive reflection" is thus consistent with a *deliberative* perspective on curriculum inquiry (see also McCutcheon, Chapter 3, this volume). Doll's third "R," *relations,* includes both "pedagogical relations . . . connections within a curriculum's structure . . . [and]

cultural relations . . . within which the curriculum is embedded," each of which complements the other; relations are continent, are "always changing," and should be "positively and communally developed" by students and teachers (p. 179). Thus, for example, "the textbook . . . is seen as something to revise, not as something to follow" (p. 180). Finally, *rigor,* in Doll's terms, "keeps a transformative curriculum from falling into either rampant relativism or sentimental solipsism" (p. 181) and "may be defined in terms of mixing—indeterminacy with interpretation" (p. 183); rigor involves "purposely looking for different alternatives, relations, [and] connections" (p. 182) and "the conscious attempt to ferret out . . . (often hidden) assumptions" in "combining . . . determinacy and indeterminacy" (p. 183).

Discussions of chaos in curriculum inquiry would be improved by the application of a little more rigor, since many to date have been characterized by an unbridled (and sometimes uncritical) enthusiasm for the work of Belgian thermodynamicist Ilya Prigogine (Prigogine & Stengers, 1984) and/or the scientists and mathematicians whose work was popularized by science journalist James Gleick in *Chaos: The Making of a New Science* (1987).[9] While I do not dispute the heuristic value of chaos in animating these discussions, I want to draw attention to some of their silences and to suggest some other issues that might be addressed. For example, can chaos theory be any more than a source of generative metaphors for curriculum work? Is it enough to say that the dynamics of curriculum are like those of self-organizing systems, or can it be shown that a curriculum *is* a complex system displaying the properties located in what science names chaos? Does this distinction really matter if the juxtaposition of chaos theory with curriculum inquiry encourages new forms of social imagination?[10]

As already noted, the dominant discourses of curriculum inquiry are characterized by metaphors that suggest closed systems and linear dynamics. Chaos and complexity theories, especially when deployed rigorously by scholars such as Doll (1993), invite us to consider the possibilities and practicalities of working in open, far-from-equilibrium systems, the dynamics of which are nonlinear, self-reflexive, irreversible, and self-organizing. However, we also need to resist the temptation to "elementarize" these characteristics—to reduce them to the elements of yet another model in which curriculum is (again) oversimplified and distorted (see Green & Bigum, 1993).

Debates about the applicability of chaos theory to curriculum inquiry often return to questions about the relationship between "natural" order and human affairs. For example, Hunter and Benson (1997) castigate MacPherson (1995) for claiming that "chaos theory . . . is a closer fit [than classical empiricism] for naturally occurring phenomena (e.g., weather) and for human endeavors (e.g., education)" (Hunter & Benson, 1997, p. 89). MacPherson, they argue,

> rejects the deterministic cause–effect reasoning of classical empiricism in favour of the indeterminate cause–effect reasoning of chaotic empiricism. In the process, MacPherson conflates the natural world and the human world. He makes the implicit assumption that there are no meaningful differences between asking questions about the weather or asking questions about education. In essence, this amounts to a claim that the study of the behaviour of sentient beings may proceed on the same assumptions and the same methods as a study of the behaviour of molecules of air. As we have argued elsewhere [citation omitted], this kind of extension of chaos theory precludes the possibility of choice or willful action by human beings and simply extends the category error previously made in applying the methods of natural science to the study of social phenomena. (p. 89)

Hunter and Benson (1997) ignore an obvious alternative, namely, that there is no sharp dichotomy between matter and life, between nature and culture. The methods of natural science are themselves "social phenomena" and, as Sandra Harding (1993) writes, "being able to explain the regularities of nature and their underlying causal tendencies is inseparable from providing the same kinds of explanations of the social relations of science" (p. 6). I agree with Hunter and Benson that we should be suspicious of any claim that "the study of the behaviour of sentient beings may proceed on the same assumptions and the same methods as a study of the behaviour of molecules of air" (p. 89), but the reverse of this proposition is much less problematic. For example, quantum physicists proceed on the assumption that something like "free will" can be attributed to the smallest particles of matter, and explicitly reject the view that physical reality can be understood as existing independently of human observation.[11] Understanding the behavior of molecules of air is inseparable from understanding the prevailing modes of representation within our culture, history, and species that lead us to imagine "molecules" in the first place. If we take the view that "nature-as-an-object-of-knowledge is always cultural" (Harding, 1993, p. 1), Hunter and Benson's "category error" disappears.[12]

However, I am prepared to admit that Hunter and Benson might be using the wrong reasons to support a defensible position. While there is no categorical reason for excluding the invocation of nature as a ground for judgment, when arguments taken from natural science are employed to support social and cultural policies and practices, we have to ask *why should descriptions of the physical world be prescriptions for social life?* Andrew

Ross (1994) sums up the issue very nicely when he writes: "Ideas that draw upon the authority of nature nearly always have their origin in ideas about society" (p. 15). More recently, Ross (1996) has used chaos theory as an explicit example of the problem to which he alludes: "Outside of *Jurassic Park,* I have yet to see a critique of Chaos Theory that fully exposes its own kinship with New Right biologism, underpinned by the flexible economic regimes of post-Fordist economics" (p. 114).[13]

According to Ross, U.S. vice president Al Gore's (1992) book, *Earth in Balance,* is a case in point. Ross (1996) reads Gore as establishing "a pervasive kinship between ecological crisis and the latest crisis of Cold War liberal consensus politics . . . however, the consensus-building machine of liberal capitalism has been thrown out of whack by the collapse of the communist threat" (p. 114). Yet chaos theory explains that the ecological crisis is natural and that it means we are moving to a higher state of equilibrium. "What Gore invites, then,"

> is this conclusion: far from owing anything to the legitimation crisis of the national security state and the permanent war economy, the latest consensus crisis of liberal capitalism should be seen as a natural event, especially since the whole world is in a state of disequilibrium—"nature is out of place." The time is now ripe for the emergence of a new stable state of world equilibrium, consciously directed by the need to rescue its natural resources. (Ross,1996, p. 114)

In other words, Gore uses popular understandings of the "naturalness" of chaos and ecological crisis to legitimate the production of a new world order that once again privileges stability and equilibrium. There is an underlying similarity between Richard Nixon (in Oliver Stone's version of history) seeing the national political system as a wild animal to be "tamed," and Al Gore seeing it as an ecosystem that needs to be "in balance." They use different metaphors for different times, but each envisions the system as having some natural qualities that provide humans with moral justifications for their interventions. Hayles (1990) provides a useful framework for understanding the widespread popularity of chaos theory at this moment in history:

> Different disciplines, sufficiently distant from one another so that direct influence seems unlikely, . . . nevertheless focus on similar kinds of problems [at] about the same time and base their formulations on isomorphic assumptions. . . . Different disciplines are drawn to similar problems because the concerns underlying them are highly charged within a prevailing cultural context. . . . Scientific theories and models are culturally conditioned, par-

taking of and rooted in assumptions that can be found at multiple sites throughout the culture. (p. xi)

Thus, the questions I want to ask about chaos and complexity theories in curriculum inquiry are concerned with exposing their "isomorphic assumptions." Why are so many different disciplines, including education, basing the theories they construct on similar presuppositions about nonlinear dynamics, turbulence, far-from-equilibrium states, strange attractors, and so on? That question remains a very open one for me, and thus I want to strenuously *resist* the impulse to see chaos and complexity theories as new paradigms for curriculum work, although I am more than happy to continue exploring the generative possibilities of the new metaphors they provide.

At the very least, the language of chaos and complexity theory encourages us to see curriculum administration as work that anticipates— and even welcomes—unpredictable change and evolution. Instead of seeing disturbances to business-as-usual as "problems" to be "solved," we can look for the new opportunities that states of disequilibrium present to us for evolution (and perhaps revolution). A homeostatic view of curriculum systems suggests that there is something intrinsically desirable about working in a state of stability and equilibrium,[14] in much the same way that a means–ends (or process–product) model of curriculum development gives us a false sense of security when we achieve our ends. We do not solve problems in curriculum work in the hope that we eventually will have fewer such problems to solve, any more than crossword puzzle addicts hope that, by completing each crossword, they are reducing the number of puzzles remaining to be solved. Certainly, as a teacher, I do not place much value on the "stable outputs" that we expect from homeostatic systems; I like to be pleasantly surprised by what my students achieve. To produce pleasant surprises in our work, we sometimes may need to deliberately induce perturbations into our systems. As noted previously, Doll's (1993) four Rs—richness, recursion, relations, and rigor— provide principled criteria for producing educative disequilibrium.

A NARRATIVE TURN

As I foreshadowed above, another alternative to acting on conservative forms of systematic rationality in curriculum work is to participate in what has come to be known as the "narrative turn" and, more recently, the "textual turn" in curriculum inquiry—where both of these "turns" are informed by the various approaches to literary and cultural studies that now tend to be labeled postmodernist and poststructuralist. Narrative theory invites us to think of all discourse as taking the form of a story, and poststructuralist theories invite us to think of all discourse as taking the form of texts. Strategically, this would entail reading curriculum documents (such as Vermont's and Victoria's *Framework* documents) as deconstructed texts. As Pinar and Reynolds (1992) write:

> Curriculum as deconstructed text acknowledges knowledge as preeminently historical. Here, however, history is not understood as ideologically constructed, rather as a series of narratives superimposed upon each other, interlaced among each other, layers of story merged and separated like the colors in Jackson Pollock's paintings. . . . To understand curriculum as a deconstructed (or deconstructing) text is to tell stories that never end, stories in which the listener, the "narratee", may become a character or indeed the narrator, in which all structure is provisional, momentary, a collection of twinkling stars in a firmament of flux. (p. 7)

According to this perspective, a curriculum document should not be read as a transmitter of essential meanings but, to quote Umberto Eco's (1984) definition of the novel, as a "machine for generating interpretations," and an appropriate role for curriculum leaders thus would be to invite other readers to go beyond a single interpretive act "to tell stories that never end" (p. 54). As Kenneth Knoespel (1991) writes, "Rather than reading a single text a single time, [deconstruction] promotes the reading of many texts many times for an ongoing confessional comprehension of how meaning is generated" (p. 116). The methodological disposition I am advocating here is characterized succinctly by the literary critic Barbara Johnson's response to an invitation to define deconstruction:

> One thing I could say is that the training most people get from the beginning, in school and through all the cultural pressures on us, is to answer the question: "What's the bottom line?" What deconstruction does is to teach you to ask: "What does the construction of the bottom line leave out? What does it repress? What does it disregard? What does it consider unimportant? What does it put in the margins?" So that it's a double process. You have to have some sense of what someone's conception of what the bottom line would be, is, in order to organise the "noise" that is being disregarded. (Quoted in Salusinsky, 1987, p. 81)

Thus, in regard to interpreting and implementing curriculum documents, curriculum leadership perhaps should be oriented toward uncovering what Johnson calls "noise"—that which is disregarded or marginalized by the dominant cultural myths and narratives that these documents typically incorporate. Deconstruction invites us to find or invent ways to destabilize texts to make them yield unexpected conclusions—generalizations (especially those based on bipolar terms) are pushed to their limits to reveal their absurdities; ambiguities and ambivalences are cultivated rather than avoided. The curriculum leader as deconstructive reader would try to make curriculum documents "behave" in unpredictable and complex ways.

For example, one of the learning outcomes specified for grades 7 and 8 in the "Studies of Society and Environment" volume of Victoria's *Framework* is that students will be able to "explain economic decisions made by governments" (Victoria, Board of Studies, 1995, p. 18). Every time I have read this outcome statement aloud to audiences of educators, they have roared with laughter at its absurdity. Yet I am sure that the authors of this outcome intended it to be taken seriously—a reading that is, indeed, possible if the statement is understood in the context of the dominant cultural myth (or perhaps I should say a myth of the dominant culture), in which governments are assumed to make rational (and maybe even wise) economic decisions. In this instance, a curriculum leader might want to explore with teachers the implications of reading this statement in different ways. Should they take the predictable route and encourage students to learn the conventional textbook explanations of economic decisions made by governments? Or should they interpret this statement in a less predictable, but perhaps more generative, way by treating it as an absurdity? I suggest that the latter alternative not only is less hypocritical for most teachers but also opens up richer and more imaginative possibilities for teaching and learning.

Vermont students in grades 7 and 8 apparently are not expected to find economic decisions made by governments to be explicable, since the one comparable reference in the Vermont *Framework* states that "understanding how governments affect the flow of resources, goods, and services" is a standard that "applies to grades 9–12 only" (Vermont, State Board of Education, 1996a, p. 6.4). Achievement of this standard is assumed to be evident when students "identify and analyze the meaning, uses, and effects of tariffs, free trade, boycotts, embargoes, currency, taxes, and monetary policies" (p. 6.4). My disposition toward reading deconstructively leads me to ask what is being marginalized or disregarded by this standard, a question given added impetus by noting that this is the *only* entry under the heading "governments and resources" within the standards for economics—or what the *Framework* describes elsewhere as "essential knowledge" and "what students should *know* . . . the most important and enduring ideas, issues, dilemmas, principles, and concepts from the disciplines" (p. i). Why, for example, is free trade privileged as an important and enduring idea, rather than alternative concepts such as *fair trade?* Again, this standard may seem unexceptional if it is read as part of a dominant cultural narrative in which free trade and fair trade are assumed to be equivalent (since free trade seems fair to the dominant cultural interests it serves).

We can, however, make this standard "behave" in a less predictable and more complex way if we juxtapose it with other standards elsewhere in the *Framework* (a strategy that is not necessarily encouraged by the document's design, which privileges a traditional disciplinary categorization of knowledge rather than interdisciplinarity). The "governments and resources" standard is listed within the History and Social Sciences Standards. However, "resources" also are mentioned in the Science, Mathematics, and Technology Standards, such as in a section on natural resources (within the Design and Technology theme), and in the following grades 5–8 standard, which appears in a section on "theories, systems, and forces" (within the Universe, Earth, and the Environment theme): "Analyze and explain natural resource management and demonstrate an understanding of the ecological interactions and interdependence between humans and their resource demands on environmental systems (e.g., waste disposal, energy resources, recycling, pollution reduction)" (p. 7.6).[15]

What would it mean to develop a curriculum in which both this and the "governments and resources" standard were mutually interreferenced rather than treated separately? I suggest that if this was done, it quickly would become apparent that "the meaning, uses, and effects of . . . free trade" is a much more complex and problematic matter than it may appear to be at first sight. For example, under the terms of the Uruguay round of the General Agreement on Tariffs and Trade (GATT) in the early 1990s, which was supported enthusiastically by the Clinton administration, many U.S. environmental laws—on emissions, recycling, waste reduction, toxic substances in packaging—can be challenged as barriers to free trade by nations with no comparable environmental legislation of their own. In other words, GATT's threat to consumer and environmental protections is part of the "noise" around the concept of free trade that may be disregarded by treating it in conventional ways. Reading the concept of free trade in conjunction with natural resource management issues may help us to uncover that "noise."

This approach to reading curriculum documents would, I suggest, be facilitated by making them available in electronic—and preferably hypertextual—forms, so that they literally could be dismantled and/or rearranged, as well as being read deconstructively (in the sense of laying their structures bare). Because digitized information is easily edited into different forms, an electronic text is not bound by the linearity of conventional narrative forms. Hypertexts appear to encourage intertextual reading and multivocal writing—an observation that is consistent with claims that electronic writing technologies converge with or embody much post-structuralist literary theory.[16] These claims should not, of course, be taken at face value, but I believe that, as curriculum documents increasingly are disseminated in electronic form, we need to understand just what is new and different about electronic authorship and readership, and to look more closely at the ways in which the networks of inscriptions that constitute electronic texts circulate within curriculum systems.

EMERGING DISPOSITIONS

How might democratic curriculum leaders use the understandings of systems I have presented here to reflect continuously and critically on their work? I first would want to emphasize that nothing in this essay should be taken as "advice," since I have not sought to *explain* systems in curriculum work but to *explore* them. I am using the term *essay* here as a verb—to attempt, to try, to test. In conceptual inquiry an essay serves a function comparable to that of the experiment in empirical research—a disciplined way of investigating a question, problem, or issue. Both *essay* and *assay* come to us through the French *essayer* from the Latin *exigere*, to weigh; I write essays to test ideas, to "weigh" them up, to give me a sense of their worth. For me, writing an essay is a form of inquiry: Most of the time, when I start to write, I do not know what the final thesis of my essay will be. Reviewing what I have written, I would suggest that what emerges from my exploration of curriculum systems is a number of *dispositions* that might be worthy of curriculum leaders' attention:

- *Metaphors matter.* We need to be aware of the metaphors we and others are using and to critically assess their appropriateness. If, like Richard Nixon, we think of the system in which we work as a wild animal to be tamed, then we may have only ourselves to blame if it turns against us.
- *Check historical baggage.* Metaphors and other concepts have complex histories that endure in the form of conceptual baggage that accompanies their circulation and reproduction in contemporary discourses. We cannot accept without question that metaphors generated in other times are appropriate for current usage. The factory model of schooling, "curriculum engineering," and the "cybernetic principle" of homeostatic self-regulation are obviously relics of another era that have passed their use-by date. We cannot assume that principles of emergence and

chaos—or even narrative theory—necessarily will be any more enduring.

- *Doubt "natural" order.* We need to be suspicious of the argument that some patterns of organization of human affairs should be privileged because they conform to some "natural" order. If chaos and complexity theories provide us with generative metaphors for thinking about organizational behavior, it is because *we make them so*, not because they appear to describe "natural" phenomena.

- *Resist regulation.* Be suspicious of regulatory devices, such as centrally produced curriculum standards and frameworks. To be suspicious of such devices does not necessarily entail rejecting them or ignoring them. They are significant cultural artifacts and quite possibly very useful as educational resources—but it is for *us* to "regulate" *them*, not vice versa.

- *Read (de)constructively.* Deconstruction is a constructive activity oriented toward revealing what is disregarded or marginalized by a text and thus making what otherwise might have been ignored available to us for productive purposes. Deconstruction helps us to destabilize and subvert regulatory texts—to make them behave in unexpected, and perhaps more generative, ways.

NOTES

1. I intend my use of "we" to include any colleagues for whom the term "democratic curriculum leadership" signifies a practice they are committed to improving.

2. I am not particularly comfortable with being positioned as a "helper." I try to heed the advice of Lila Watson, an Australian Aboriginal educator and activist, who is reported as saying, "If you've come to help me you're wasting your time. But if you've come because your liberation is bound up with mine, then let's work together" (Wadsworth, 1991, p. 11). I initially was attracted to participating in this book project because it was envisioned that we would be working *with* curriculum leaders rather than seeking to "help" them.

3. I have been inspired here by Michel Foucault's (1969/1972) archaeological approach to social inquiry, but I do not claim to be exemplifying his method.

4. Indeed, I suspect that the contrary is more plausible, especially if we take into account the many cultural and historical differences between these states that affect the governance of education within them.

5. Smith, Stanley, and Shores (1957) also had a chapter titled "Curriculum Development as Educational Engineering" in their influential text, *Fundamentals of Curriculum Development* (first published in 1951 and revised in 1957), and Beauchamp's first edition of *Curriculum Theory*, published in 1961, thus might be seen

to be following in their footsteps. But on the evidence provided by his 1968 edition, it would seem that Beauchamp remained thoroughly insulated from the social and political consciousness raising that characterized the 1960s in most Western industrial democracies. Fortunately, not all curriculum theorists were tarred with Beauchamp's brush, as Joseph Schwab (1969a) demonstrated a year later with the publication of *College Curricula and Student Protest*.

6. Critics of mechanistic curriculum models included the "deliberative" curriculum scholars for whom Schwab's (1969b, 1971, 1973) papers on "the practical" were seminal, together with the authors (and their affiliates) represented in the edited collection, *Curriculum Theorizing: The Reconceptualists* (Pinar, 1975). The latter included not only scholars using the phenomenological methods favored by William Pinar and Madeleine Grumet (1976), but also those who adopted a critical social science (and often neo-Marxist) perspective in educational inquiry, notably Michael Apple (1979) and Samuel Bowles and Herbert Gintis (1976).

7. An irreverent but revealing commentary on the genesis of cyberwords is offered by the computer scientist and science fiction author Rudy Rucker (1994): "The funny thing about the 'cyber' prefix was that it had always meant bullshit. Back in the 1940s, the story went, MIT doubledome Norbert Wiener had wanted a title for a book he'd written about the electronic control of machines. Claude Shannon, also known as The Father of Information Theory, told Wiener to call his book *Cybernetics*. The academic justification for the word was that the 'cyber' root came from the Greek word for 'rudder.' A 'kybernetes' was a steersman, or, by extension, a mechanical governor such as a weight-and-pulley feedback device you might hook to your tiller to keep your sailboat aimed at some fixed angle into the wind. The practical justification for the word was contained in Shannon's advice to Wiener: 'Use the word *cybernetics*, Norbert, because nobody knows what it means. This will always put you at an advantage in arguments'" (p. 19).

8. Such conceptions of "natural" order are pervasive in many different disciplines, including the science of ecology, which, during the postwar period and under the leadership of Eugene Odum, privileged the concept of the ecosystem as a stable and enduring emblem of natural order. As Donald Worster (1995) points out, the several editions of Odum's (1971) textbook, *Fundamentals of Ecology*, "laid so much stress on natural order that it came close to dehistoricizing nature altogether" (p. 70). Elsewhere, Worster (1993) describes in detail the ways in which, over the past 2 decades, ecologists have repudiated Odum's portrayal of orderly and predictable processes of ecological succession culminating in stable ecosystems. For example, the essays collected by Pickett and White (1985) deliver the consistent message that the very concept of the ecosystem has receded in usefulness, and to the extent that the word *ecosystem* remains in use, it has lost its former implications of order and equilibrium.

9. Gleick attends closely to the work of (for example) Mitchell Feigenbaum, Edward Lorenz, Benoit Mandelbrot, and the Santa Cruz collective but, curiously, virtually ignores Prigogine. It also should be noted that MacPherson (1995) totally ignores Prigogine (as he similarly ignores Doll, Ennis, and Sawada & Caley).

10. There are also tensions between the institutional implications of "scientific" chaos and complexity theories and an understanding of curriculum as a de-

constructed text (see Gough, 1994; Pinar & Reynolds, 1992). Chaos theory raises expectations of being the basis for a new foundational synthesis (a metanarrative, a culturally dominant myth), while deconstruction subverts universalizing systems and discourses. That is, poststructuralism challenges the impulse to write a metanarrative of chaos that is immanent in the (re)presentation of chaos theory as the harbinger of a new scientific/cultural paradigm. This is not to deny the complementarity of the destabilizing methods made available by both deconstruction and chaos theory, but it does suggest a need for caution in "emplotting" chaos in curriculum-as-text.

11. Indeed, without a sentient observer, quantum mechanics would have nothing to say about the universe. This is true for all natural sciences, of course, but quantum physicists are more explicit, even going so far as to suggest that consciousness is a necessary (and perhaps sufficient) condition for the existence of the universe.

12. Hunter and Benson's "category error" also disappears if we accept the poststructuralist proposition that there is no "outside" of the text, no "reality" that we can separate from its textual (or discursive) production. This works both ways, by accepting not only the materiality of discourse but also the agency of nature and other objects of the world "out there." Stacy Alaimo (1994) suggests that conceiving nature as artifactual, as co-constructed by humans and nonhumans, reduces the risk of "a wholesale appropriation of nature by culture" since this allows us to recognize the agency of nature "without personifying it into a mirror of human actions" (pp. 146–147).

13. Like Social Darwinism before it, "New Right biologism" refers to a selective and strategic deployment of biological ideas in the pursuit of conservative political and economic goals. Like biotechnology, applied research in chaotic and complex systems has attracted considerable government and commercial support, and Ross invites us to critically examine the motives for such support. Similarly, chaos theory may be attractive to free-market economists who champion global economic integration and deregulation, which contrasts with national development models in which the agricultural and industrial sectors of a nation's economy are regulated and articulated internally. Rather than national economies built from networks of interlocking primary and secondary industrial assembly lines, post-Fordism promotes a global market in which efficiencies are achieved through, for example, farm concentration and specialization.

14. I also suggest that we should not fear being accused of advocating change for the sake of change; this cliché obscures its own emptiness. If we "read" change in this way, I would suggest that we are not being active enough as readers.

15. An identical statement appears for grades 9–12 with "production, consumption" as the parenthetical examples.

16. See Ilana Snyder (1996) for a useful summary of these arguments.

REFERENCES

Alaimo, S. (1994). Cyborg and feminist interventions: Challenges for an environmental feminism. *Feminist Studies, 20*(1), 133–152.

Apple, M. W. (1979). *Ideology and curriculum*. London: Routledge.

Beauchamp, G. A. (1968). *Curriculum theory* (2nd ed.). Wilmette, IL: Kagg Press.

Boomer, G. (1982). Ten strategies for good teaching. In G. Boomer (Ed.), *Negotiating the curriculum* (pp. 119–121). Gosford, New South Wales: Ashton Scholastic.

Bowles, S., & Gintis, H. (1976). *Schooling in capitalist America: Educational reform and the contradictions of economic life*. New York: Basic Books.

Doll, W. E. (1986). Prigogine: A new sense of order, a new curriculum. *Theory into Practice, 25*(1), 10–16.

Doll, W. E. (1989). Foundations for a post-modern curriculum. *Journal of Curriculum Studies, 21*(3), 243–253.

Doll, W. E. (1993). *A post-modern perspective on curriculum*. New York: Teachers College Press.

Doll, W. E., & Alcazar, A. (1998). Curriculum and concepts of control. In W. F. Pinar (Ed.), *Curriculum: Toward new identities* (pp. 295–323). New York: Garland.

Eco, U. (1984). *Postscript to the name of the rose* (W. Weaver, Trans.). New York: Harcourt Brace and Jovanovich.

Ennis, C. D. (1992). Reconceptualizing learning as a dynamical system. *Journal of Curriculum and Supervision, 7*(2), 115–130.

Foucault, M. (1972). *The archeology of knowledge* (A. M. S. Smith, Trans.). New York: Pantheon. (Original work published 1969)

Gibson, W. (1984). *Neuromancer*. New York: Ace.

Giedion, S. (1948). *Mechanization takes command: A contribution to anonymous history*. New York: Oxford University Press.

Gleick, J. (1987). *Chaos: The making of a new science*. New York: Viking.

Gore, A. (1992). *Earth in balance: Ecology and the human spirit*. New York: Houghton Mifflin.

Gough, N. (1994). Imagining an erroneous order: Understanding curriculum as phenomenological and deconstructed text. *Journal of Curriculum Studies, 26*(5), 553–568.

Gough, N. (1995). Manifesting cyborgs in curriculum inquiry. *Melbourne Studies in Education, 29*(1), 71–83.

Green, B., & Bigum, C. (1993). Governing chaos: Postmodern science, information technology, and educational administration. *Educational Philosophy and Theory, 25*(2), 79–103.

Grumet, M. R. (1981). Restitution and reconstruction of educational experience: An autobiographical method for curriculum theory. In M. Lawn & L. Barton (Eds.), *Rethinking curriculum studies: A radical approach* (pp. 115–130). London: Croom Helm.

Haraway, D. J. (1991). *Simians, cyborgs, and women: The reinvention of nature*. New York: Routledge.

Harding, S. (Ed.). (1993). *The "racial" economy of science: Toward a democratic future*. Bloomington and Indianapolis: Indiana University Press.

Hayles, N. K. (1990). *Chaos bound: Orderly disorder in contemporary literature and science*. Ithaca, NY: Cornell University Press.

Hayles, N. K. (1994). Boundary disputes: Homeostasis, reflexivity, and the foundations of cybernetics. *Configurations: A Journal of Literature, Science, and Technology, 2*(3), 441–467.

Hunkins, F. P. (1980). *Curriculum development: Program improvement.* Columbus, OH: Merrill.

Hunter, W. J., & Benson, G. D. (1997). Arrows in time: The misapplication of chaos theory to education. *Journal of Curriculum Studies, 29*(1), 87–100.

Knoespel, K. J. (1991). The emplotment of chaos: Instability and narrative order. In N. K. Hayles (Ed.), *Chaos and order: Complex dynamics in literature and science* (pp. 100–122). Chicago: University of Chicago Press.

MacPherson, E. D. (1995). Chaos in the curriculum. *Journal of Curriculum Studies, 27*(3), 263–279.

McLuhan, M. (1951). *The mechanical bride: Folklore of industrial man.* New York: Vanguard Press.

Odum, E. P. (1971). *Fundamentals of ecology* (3rd ed.). Philadelphia: W. B. Saunders.

Pickett, S.T.A., & White, P. S. (Eds.). (1985). *The ecology of natural disturbance and patch dynamics.* Orlando, FL: Academic Press.

Pinar, W. F. (Ed.). (1975). *Curriculum theorizing: The reconceptualists.* Berkeley: McCutchan.

Pinar, W. F., & Grumet, M. R. (1976). *Toward a poor curriculum.* Dubuque, IA: Kendall/Hunt.

Pinar, W. F., & Reynolds, W. M. (Eds.). (1992). *Understanding curriculum as phenomenological and deconstructed text.* New York: Teachers College Press.

Pratt, D. (1980). *Curriculum: Design and development.* New York: Harcourt Brace Jovanovich.

Prigogine, I., & Stengers, I. (1984). *Order out of chaos: Man's new dialogue with nature.* New York: Bantam.

Ross, A. (1994). *The Chicago gangster theory of life: Nature's debt to society.* London and New York: Verso.

Ross, A. (1996). Earth to Gore, Earth to Gore. In S. Aronowitz, B. Martinsons, M. Menser, & J. Rich (Eds.), *Technoscience and cyberculture* (pp. 111–121). New York and London: Routledge.

Rucker, R. (1994). *The hacker and the ants.* New York: Avon Books.

Salusinsky, I. (1987). *Criticism in society.* New York and London: Methuen.

Sawada, D., & Caley, M. T. (1985). Dissipative structures: New metaphors for becoming in education. *Educational Researcher, 14*(3), 13–19.

Schwab, J. J. (1969a). *College curricula and student protest.* Chicago: University of Chicago Press.

Schwab, J. J. (1969b). The practical: A language for curriculum. *School Review, 78*(1), 1–23.

Schwab, J. J. (1971). The practical: Arts of eclectic. *School Review, 79*(4), 493–542.

Schwab, J. J. (1973). The practical 3: Translation into curriculum. *School Review, 81*(4), 501–522.

Smith, B. O., Stanley, W. O., & Shores, J. H. (1957). *Fundamentals of curriculum development* (rev. ed.). New York: Harcourt, Brace & World.

Snyder, I. (1996). *Hypertext: The electronic labyrinth.* Carlton, Victoria: Melbourne University Press.

Taylor, F. W. (1947). *Scientific management.* New York: Harper and Brothers. (Original work published 1911)

Vermont, State Board of Education. (1996a). *Vermont's framework of standards and learning opportunities.* Montpelier: Vermont Department of Education.

Vermont, State Board of Education. (1996b). *Core connections: A how-to guide for using Vermont's framework.* Montpelier: Vermont Department of Education.

Victoria, Board of Studies. (1995). *Curriculum and standards framework.* Carlton, Victoria: Board of Studies.

Wadsworth, Y. (1991). *Everyday evaluation on the run.* Melbourne: Action Research Issues Association.

Worster, D. (1993). *The wealth of nature: Environmental history and the ecological imagination.* New York: Oxford University Press.

Worster, D. (1995). Nature and the disorder of history. In M. E. Soulé & G. Lease (Eds.), *Reinventing nature? Responses to postmodern deconstruction* (pp. 65–85). Washington, DC: Island Press.

Critical Democracy and Education

JOE L. KINCHELOE

THE ACADEMIC TRADITION I come from often is referred to as the school of *critical theory.* It usually refers to the theoretical tradition developed by the Frankfurt School, a group of scholars connected to the Institute of Social Research at the University of Frankfurt in Germany. Max Horkheimer, Theodor Adorno, and Herbert Marcuse initiated a conversation with the German tradition of philosophical and social thought, particularly the work of Marx, Kant, Hegel, and Weber. From the vantage point of these critical theorists, whose political sensibilities were influenced by the devastation of World War I, postwar Germany with its economic depression marked by inflation and unemployment, as well as the failed strikes and protests in Germany and throughout Central Europe during this same period, the world was in urgent need of reinterpretation. From this perspective, they defied Marxist orthodoxy while deepening their belief that injustice and subjugation shaped the lived world (Bottomore, 1984; Gibson, 1984; Held, 1980; Jay, 1973). Focusing their attention on the changing nature of capitalism, the early critical theorists analyzed the mutating forms of domination that accompanied this change (Giroux, 1983; Kincheloe & McLaren, 1994; McLaren, 1994).

Many academicians who had come of age in the politically charged atmosphere of the 1960s focused their scholarly attention on critical theory. Frustrated by forms of domination emerging from a post-Enlightenment culture nurtured by capitalism, these scholars saw in critical theory a method of temporarily freeing academic work from these forms of power. Making use of critical theory's concern with the way

Understanding Democratic Curriculum Leadership. Copyright © 1999 by Teachers College, Columbia University. All rights reserved. ISBN 0-8077-3826-3 (pbk), ISBN 0-8077-3827-1 (cloth). Prior to photocopying items for classroom use, please contact the Copyright Clearance Center, Customer Service, 222 Rosewood Dr., Danvers, MA 01923, USA, tel. (508) 750-8400.

power worked to shape individual consciousness and ways of seeing—
the social construction of experience—these young scholars came to view
their academic disciplines as manifestations of the discourses and power
relations of the social and historical contexts that produced them. The
"discourse of possibility" implicit within the constructed nature of social
experience suggested to these scholars that a reconstruction of the social
sciences could help foster a more egalitarian and democratic social order.
New conceptualizations of human agency promising that men and
women could, in part, determine their own existence, offered new hope
for emancipatory forms of social practice when compared with orthodox
Marxism's assertion of the iron jaws of history, the irrevocable evil of
capitalism, and the proletariat as the privileged subject and anticipated
agent of social transformation. For example, when Henry Giroux and
other critical educators criticized the argument made by Marxist scholars
Samuel Bowles and Herbert Gintis that schools were capitalist agencies of
social, economic, cultural, and bureaucratic reproduction, they contrasted
the deterministic perspectives of Bowles and Gintis with the idea that
schools, as venues of hope, could become sites of resistance and democratic possibility through concerted efforts among teachers and students
to work within a liberatory pedagogical framework. Giroux (1983), in
particular, maintained that schools could become institutions where
forms of knowledge, values, and social relations were taught for the purpose of educating young people for critical empowerment rather than
subjugation.

CRITICAL DEMOCRATIC THEORY AND EDUCATION

While many other traditions have merged with the Frankfurt School to
produce contemporary forms of critical theory, constraints of space preclude detailed discussion of this topic. Suffice it to say that continental
European theorists such as Foucault, Habermas, and Derrida; Latin American thinkers such as Paulo Freire; French feminists such as Irigaray, Kris-
teva, and Cixous; and Russian sociolinguists such as Bakhtin and Vygot-
sky all have contributed to what we think of as contemporary *critical
democratic theory.* This critical theorizing is especially concerned with how
democracy is subverted, domination takes place, and human relations are
shaped in the schools, in other cultural sites of pedagogy, and in everyday
life. Critical theorists want to promote an individual's consciousness
of himself or herself as a social being. An individual who has gained
such a consciousness understands how and why his or her political opin-

ions, worker role, religious beliefs, gender role, and racial self-image are shaped by dominant perspectives.

Critical theory, thus, promotes self-reflections that result in changes of perspective. Men and women come to know themselves by bringing to consciousness the process by which their viewpoints are formed. Strategies that can be taken to confront individual and social pathologies can be negotiated once self-reflection takes place. Critical theory is quick to point out that such strategies do not take the form of rules and precise regulations. Instead, a framework of principles is developed around which possible actions can be discussed and analyzed. Teachers who are conversant with critical theory are never certain of the exact path of action they will take as a result of their analysis. This can be quite frustrating to those raised in a modernist tradition (Cartesian–Newtonian science) that values scientifically validated certainty. Often practitioners educated in this modernist context grow accustomed to expert-produced sets of official procedures designed to direct their actions.

Critical pedagogy is the term used to describe what emerges when critical theory encounters education. Like critical theory in general, critical pedagogy refuses to delineate a specific set of teaching procedures. Critical pedagogues confront the modernist/positivist ways of seeing that dominate traditional liberal and conservative critiques of schooling (McLaren, 1994). Moving beyond these analytical forms, critical pedagogy, by exposing student sorting processes and power involvement with curriculum, helps students and teachers understand how schools work. In this way, the tradition provides teachers with insights about education that they would find nowhere else. This unique perspective is central to the importance of critical pedagogy.

Advocates of critical pedagogy make no pretense of neutrality. Unlike those following many other educational approaches, critical theorists expose their values and openly work to achieve them. Critical pedagogy is dedicated to the notion of egalitarianism and the elimination of human suffering. What is the relationship between social inequality and the suffering that accompanies it, and the schooling process? The search for an answer to this question shapes the activities of the critical teacher. Working in solidarity with subordinated and marginalized groups, critical teachers attempt to expose the subtle and often hidden educational processes that privilege the already affluent and undermine the efforts of the poor. When American schooling is viewed from this perspective, the naive belief that such education provides consistent socioeconomic mobility for working-class students disintegrates. Indeed, the notion that education simply provides a politically neutral set of skills and an objective body of knowledge also collapses. In critical pedagogy the curriculum becomes a dynamic of negotiation where students and teachers examine the forces that have shaped them and the society in which they live. In this context the curriculum is ever changing and evolving, as it seeks to uncover how the world operates and how egalitarian democratic principles can become a part of that operation. Thus, a critical curriculum attempts to engage students in the understanding and implementation of a critical democracy grounded in concerns for community building and social justice.

CRITICAL DEMOCRACY AS A WAY OF LIFE

When the concept of a critical democracy intersects with teaching, three issues emerge: (1) teaching in a democratic workplace—teacher self-direction/empowerment; (2) the creation of democratic classrooms—developing student input into the nature of their own education; and (3) teaching for democratic citizenship—building a democratic society. The following discussion of these issues rests on the philosophical assumption that democracy has to do with more than voting, that instead it is a way of life. As a way of life, it produces a set of principles on which institutions, schools in particular, are constructed. In this context democracy is a value system, a method of associating with one another, a way of confronting problems together within the boundaries of solidarity, and a means of validating human dignity.

Such a value system grounds a notion of "good work"—for laborers in general and teachers in particular. Good work is a democratic act operating in a free and autonomous workplace. It is self-creating and dedicated to critical forms of change. Good work transforms self and world, as it strives to preserve democratic ideals. Work as a democratic expression is obligated to resist those often hidden manifestations of power that subvert good work (Brosio, 1985, 1994). When administrators squash intellectual and moral freedom, freedom of inquiry, freedom of association in or out of the workplace, or freedom of religion, democratic workers do not sit still. Because such antidemocratic actions take place at a covert level unrecognized by the public, democratic workers must refine carefully their resistance strategies in order to effectively expose the insidious nature of power. For example, the antidemocratic workings of power often take place in the ostensibly neutral medium of personnel administration. Democratic workers must have the insight to expose alternative meanings of the administration's attempt to increase "human efficiency," to develop "proper work habits," to "improve morale," and to "reduce conflict." All of these goals sound sensible and benign, but all implicitly carry particular views of the arrangements of the workplace and the role of workers. To resist this form of manipulation, critical workers must gain the power to analyze texts in such a way that hidden meanings become part of the public conversation about work. As a democratic expression, good work alerts the public to the way words are deployed to mystify and confuse, to maintain unequal power relations.

When educators take such a notion to heart, the deskilling of teachers by top-down management forms no longer can afflict the profession, and the goals of teaching will begin to change. Critical democratic teachers, acting on this imperative, take on the task of redefining authority in a way that rejects hierarchical divisions of labor that serve to disempower teachers and students. Challenging the hierarchies of schooling, teachers point out that educational administration is taught only to people who serve at the head of the administrative structure and not to people who are to be administered. Ideas about democratic forms of management are not concepts that typically are discussed between principals and teachers or teachers and students. Without the awareness produced by such discussion, the social ambiance of the school remains within an authoritarian frame. The ideological web formed by this authoritarianism produces a curriculum that teaches teachers and students how to think and act in the world. Both teachers and students are taught to conform, to adjust to their inequality and their particular rung on the status ladder, and to submit to authority. Teachers and students are induced to develop an authority of dependence, a view of citizenship that is passive, a view of learning that means listening. The predisposition to question the authority structure of the school and the curriculum it teaches or to reject the image of the future that the structure presents to teachers and students is out-of-bounds. The politics of authoritarianism rubs democratic impulses the wrong way (Shor, 1992).

CRISIS OF DEMOCRACY

At the end of the twentieth century, teachers who are dedicated to the tenets of critical pedagogy and its emphasis on a critical democracy face special challenges. The last quarter of the twentieth century has been marked by a crisis of democracy—a crisis seldom referenced in the public conversation or in educational institutions. The crisis has been initiated by a growing imbalance of power and a perverted concept of neutrality that undermines analysis of the crisis. Critical educators understand that the development of new technologies over the past couple of decades has not created a new era of power sharing. Dedicated to a critical democracy, such educators have watched as corporate power wielders employ data banks, radio and TV transmissions, movies, computerization, and the Internet to promote their interests, and to create an information environment that eliminates challenges to their conception of the world. The process takes place in a quiet and subtle way, as values such as competitive individualism, the superiority of an unregulated market economy (a neoclassical economics), and the necessity of consumption are promoted implicitly. People's identities, their sense of who they are, begin to be formed not in their communities as much as by their radios and televisions. The popularity of video compilations of old 1950s and 1960s TV commercials and the emotions they trigger within those of us who grew up in that era are evidence of this media-based identity formation (Brosio, 1994; Kellner, 1990; McLaren, Hammer, Reilly, & Sholle, 1995; Smart, 1992).

It is important for educators to understand that this shaping of public opinion by way of media control is never simplistic. Many times efforts to manipulate opinion backfire, as men and women perceive what is happening to them and rebel. Also, technologies such as computer links and information highways can be used to convey alternative messages that challenge corporate control. Still, most Americans are unable to comprehend the degree of influence corporate leaders attain as they control TV and other media that bypass reason and focus directly on the management of human feelings and emotions. Media presentations that are not obviously political play to our emotions on a level that shapes our political perspectives. Images of children exuberant as they open gifts on Christmas morning have no overt political message. At the deeper level, however, such images may be influential, as they tell us that such happiness in our children can be evoked only by the consumption of goods and services. If we truly love our children and want to see them happy, then we must support the interests of the corporations that produce these valuable products. The process of political opinion formation is not a linear, rational procedure but is grounded on our emotional hopes and fears. Thus, when Mattel calls for lower corporate taxes and a better business climate in which to produce its toys, we accede to its wishes. After all, this is the company that allows us to make our children happy (Harvey, 1989; McLaren, Hammer, Reilly, & Sholle, 1995).

In addition to this power disparity, a false notion of neutrality exists in schools that impedes our ability as teachers to address such fundamental issues, such basic threats to democracy. In this pseudo-neutral culture of positivism, schooling is depicted as an objective purveyor of truth. In such a culture, educators ignore the social construction of knowledge and the dramatic role that forces of power play in knowledge construction. As an institution schooling fails to understand that one of the most important exercises of power in a postmodern world involves the prerogative to define meanings and to specify what knowledge is valuable. Without a critical resistance, knowledge becomes oppression—oppression of non-Whites, the poor, and women. Knowledge that is "totalized" has been unified into a master narrative with the intent of assuming power and seizing control. The values of the power groups that produce and validate or repress and invalidate knowledge are hidden in the culture of positivism.

An understanding of this culture of positivism is central to the success of any critical form of education. The culture of positivism operates in a way that views the world without the benefit of the social, cultural, and political context that gives reality its meaning. Positivism is an epistemology, a way of producing knowledge that privileges the logic and methods of investigation of the natural sciences. Hermeneutical (interpretive) principles of meaning making hold little status in this positivistic culture. Explanation, prediction, and technical control take on unprecedented importance—what we believe constitutes a desirable state of affairs, a good education, or an ethical citizen is of little consequence here. Thus, the culture of positivism represents the retreat of modernist science from even Western civilization's humanistic tradition, going back to the ancient Greeks, who viewed scholarship as a means of freeing oneself from uninformed opinion in order to better pursue ethical action. Space constraints preclude discussion of non-Western epistemological traditions that tie knowledge production to spiritual ways of living and ethical behavior in the community; however, this critical topic will be discussed in Chapter 6.

Positivistic culture presents a view of education and knowledge production that has little use for the critical goals of individuals deciding their own meanings, ordering their own experiences, or struggling against the sociopolitical forces that would squash their efforts toward such self-direction. By dismissing the importance of human empowerment, the culture of positivism ignores ethical and moral questions and thus tacitly supports forms of domination, hierarchy, and control. In this context knowledge produced is an external body of data that exists independent of human beings and their historical context. As it is provided to educators, such knowledge becomes a meaningless body of isolated facts to be committed to memory by overwhelmed and baffled students. Many teachers who ask students to escape this culture of positivism and engage with contextualized, personally significant, conceptual learning often find their pupils initially baffled by the purpose of such a pedagogy. They have grown comfortable in the meaningless memory rituals of a positivistic education. In this context critical teachers' efforts to discuss the process by which truth is constructed—the role of power in the production of so-called "objective data"—are viewed as flagrant attempts to politicize the neutral curriculum. Since school knowledge, many educational leaders trapped in the culture of positivism argue, has been produced in a value-free manner, it should be immune from political questioning.

If any questions about the role of power in knowledge production and curricular formation are out-of-bounds in school settings, then the political battle has been won that *education exists to provide uncritical support for the status quo.* Few flinch when they hear political and educational leaders argue that we must keep politics out of education. When we begin to understand the inseparability of political and educational questions, we contend that educators should be made more political—that we should expose the hidden politics of neutrality and the culture of positivism that supports it (Giroux, 1997; Lyotard, 1984; Scholes, 1982). Within this culture questions of efficiency and hyperrationality drive educational purpose, not questions of what knowledge is of most worth and what kind of education makes for moral citizens. This emphasis on efficiency and hyperrationality serves to fragment the world to the point that individuals are blinded to the possibility of the Frankfurt School's notion of immanent critique—the analysis of "what is" vis-à-vis "what should be." The cult of efficiency and hyperrationality studies the world in isolation, bit by bit, in the process separating the economy from human beings, the schools from society, the students from their socioeconomic backgrounds. The knowledge produced in these contexts is neutered in a way that neutralizes its power to address the crisis of democracy.

Another way education is connected to the crisis of democracy involves the vilification of the public sector of society and the sanctification of the private domain. The private sector provides the good things of life, while the public sphere gives us only headaches, taxes, bureaucrats, and red tape. The result of such a fragmentation of society manifests itself in social pathologies that undermine the quality of everyone's lives. Americans who live in urban areas, for example, are confronted by high-cost housing and traffic jams. Everyone who can afford it buys an upscale house with no concern for supplying low-income housing to those who need it in the community. The cost of housing thus is inflated as the affluent become slaves of their mortgages and the poor become homeless. As urban commuters think only of driving private cars to work, they spend more hours on congested highways breathing exhaust-filled air. The thought of working for better public transportation never crosses their mind. With the right-wing polarization of the public and private realms, the rich fashion private compounds, patrolled by private police, designed to remove them as far as possible from the decaying and ever more dangerous public sphere (Bellah et al., 1991; Home, 1986).

Schools have played a special role in their redefinition of the private and public spheres. The public role of schooling as a training ground for democracy and democratic citizenship has been substituted for a private corporate view of the role of education. In addition to their role as supplier of "adjusted labor" to the corporate machine, schools have come to be seen as commodities subject to the dictates of the market. Thus, we have witnessed the proliferation of private educational ventures, including the Disney schools and Channel One. In this milieu students are transformed from citizens to consumers, capable of being bought and sold. In this hyperreality of the private, we "consume" our young. All this talk of privatization is couched in the language of public improvement and democratic virtue. The public sphere has failed, the mystifiers argue. The private market is a much more effective mechanism in the attempt to achieve socioeconomic improvement. This return to neoclassical economics holds serious consequences. Human destiny is couched in the imagery of a football game or an air raid over Baghdad. Market forces of competition govern the world, degrading those nations and those peoples who start with an economic disadvantage. These nations' and peoples' subsequent poor performance in "the game" is chalked up to poor preparation or inferior ability. In other words, they failed for the same reasons that the Pittsburgh Steelers lost to the Miami Dolphins—bad planning, the inferiority of the offensive line. Be good sports, people; don't make excuses for your educational and economic failures (Block, 1990; Chesneaux, 1992; Macedo, 1994).

CRITICAL DEMOCRACY AS AN ETHICAL
BENCHMARK FOR EDUCATION

Critical educators use this understanding of the crisis of democracy to ground their pedagogy. Viewing their practice as the rewriting of the world, the making of a new history, and the revitalization of the democratic impulse, such educators use democracy as a benchmark for the conceptualization of school purpose. In this context critical teachers construct a system of meaning that alerts us to the workings of power and the ways in which it shapes our consciousness. Critical theorists traditionally have referred to this freeing process as emancipation or empowerment. Emancipation always involves confrontation with the forces that have shaped our consciousness. Such a confrontation allows us to glimpse who we want to be, as we struggle to understand how we have come to see the world. In our emancipatory journey toward self-direction, we can engage in a "poststructuralist critique" that alerts us to the complexity of the task. This critique helps critical teachers understand that human identity involves such a chaotic flow of intertwined forces that no social agent ever can completely disentangle himself or herself from it. Using Michael Foucault's concept of genealogy, which involves the historical process of tracing and understanding the formation of our identities, we begin to see ourselves at various points in the web of reality. We are ever confined by our placement but liberated by our appreciation of our predicament. Thus, in the spirit of this poststructuralist critique, we begin to understand and disengage ourselves from the social, political, and educational structures that shape us. We begin to expose the cultural stories (the metanarratives) that have grounded dominant ways of making sense of the world in general and education in particular. Our ability to see from a variety of perspectives forms the basis of a conversation about the unstated assumptions of the culture (a metadialogue) with ourselves. This metadialogue with ourselves continues, hopefully, for the rest of our lives and leads to a perpetual redefinition of both self and world. Such a process constitutes a radical democratic way of knowing.

Critical teachers, operating in this democratic and introspective confrontation with power, understand that self-directed education undertaken by self-organized community groups is the most powerful form of pedagogy. Teacher education in this context becomes a "prodemocracy" movement that attempts to promote forms of thinking and action that retrieve the impetus for educational change from business and industrial elites. Grounded on a conception of solidarity with the oppressed and the excluded, teacher education seeks to connect with democratic organizations dedicated to a cultural politics of emancipatory change. Here teachers and students can become part of social movements where they can employ their research and pedagogical skills to build new forms of democratic consciousness and counterhegemonic action. Such critically informed practice, or *praxis,* can revolutionize the view of knowledge as an entity produced by experts in remote locales. Postmodern knowledge becomes a product of democratic cooperation, a manifestation of what happens when experience is interrogated in the light of historical consciousness.

Engaging a student in a critical role involves the cultivation of a sophisticated form of thinking based on an active engagement with the assumptions and symbols of the culture. Understanding the shallowness of the argument that democratic citizenship involves the uncritical acquisition of a neutral body of traditional knowledge, critical teachers can connect democratic precepts with insights already present in students' experiences. Such teachers understand, in the spirit of John Dewey, that a democratic public is not a static entity, for it is always in the process of defining and redefining itself. When students are simply filled with predigested facts about the society, with unexamined social knowledge, the self-formation process is impeded. What too many mainstream educators fail to understand is that the debate over social meaning is a consummate democratic act; indeed, the public is actually created in the process of debate, in the struggle to assign meaning to tradition and its impact on the present. The Deweyan vision of the relationship between curriculum and tradition is extended by Mikhail Bakhtin's notion of *dialogism*—the process of viewing a text as a space where multiple voices and perspectives intersect. In this critical democratic education, traditions become "texts" in which various voices and traditions intersect. When critical teachers grasp this dialogism, they expand their ability to think as citizens who discover new dimensions in tradition, particularly as embodied in the given curriculum. Such individuals come to understand the tacit forces of oppression, in the process of discovering social possibilities never before considered (Feinberg, 1989; Greene, 1988, 1995).

Critical pedagogy enlightened by poststructuralist and feminist scholarship holds so much promise for teachers. I am often troubled, however, by the lack of communication that occurs between critical educational theorists and teachers. Such problems occur when theorists think in terms of educational purpose without accounting for the daily tribulations that practicing teachers must face. In this context these thoughts about critical pedagogy and democracy have been written as a discussion of purpose, what constitutes our ultimate goals as progressive teachers. In no way, therefore, do I assume an unproblematic effort to translate such goals into everyday teaching.

Teachers (myself included) face a myriad of structural and interpersonal impediments to any easy process of making these ideas come alive in the classroom. Yet, miraculously, many are able to make the process work year after year. Hopefully, this dialogue between pedagogical purpose and the limiting forces of educational institutions will enhance all of our capacities to accomplish the critical democratic goals delineated here.

FRAMEWORK OF PRINCIPLES: CRITICAL
DEMOCRACY AND HERMENEUTICS

As Jim Henderson writes in Chapter 1, curriculum leaders need to enter into the interpretive and meaning-making dynamics of the hermeneutical circle. I will conclude this chapter in the context of Henderson's appeal. My chapter has made use of a normative hermeneutics that raises questions about the purposes of interpretation. In its critical theory-driven manner, the hermeneutics employed here provides an understanding of a variety of cultural and pedagogical issues in light of larger political processes. In this context this critical hermeneutics develops a form of cultural criticism that sets the stage for transformative action. As critical hermeneuts engage in this task, they study the ways in which interpretations are socially situated, the ways in which individuals make meaning within conceptual structures they have not necessarily chosen for themselves. Understanding this, critical hermeneuts in education real-ize that a central aspect of their work involves unraveling the political inscriptions embedded in pedagogical texts. This unraveling is compli-cated by the taken-for-grantedness of the meanings promoted in these representations and the typically undetected ways these representations are circulated into everyday life (Denzin & Lincoln, 1994; Steinberg, 1998; Steinberg & Kincheloe, 1997).

In this hermeneutical context this chapter has promoted a frame-work of 10 critical principles that help educators make sense of the tacit ways power operates to shape education. Supported by these understand-ings, curriculum leaders can develop transformative practices. The 10 principles are as follows:

1. The necessity of analyzing the ways in which power produces academic disciplines that undermine democracy
2. The importance of critical self-reflection concerning the con-struction of one's consciousness that results in self-direction and community building
3. The process of developing a democratic way of knowing that helps free teachers and students from the effects of social injus-tice and subjugation
4. The need to expose educational processes that privilege the priv-ileged
5. The value of creating good work for teachers and eluding op-pressive forms of administration
6. The worthiness of gaining the power to analyze texts promoting the crisis of democracy
7. The priority of exposing false notions of neutrality that exacer-bate social control and oppression
8. The significance of the vilification of the public sector as part of a larger power play
9. The benefit of disengaging ourselves from repressive power alli-ances and the knowledge they produce
10. The worth of finding social and pedagogical possibilities never before considered

All of these critical principles rest on this text's hermeneutic vision. Underlying this vision is the assumption that curriculum leaders have the facility to grasp and display the connections among educational practice, everyday life, communications processes, cultural patterns, and the formation of human consciousness. In many contemporary schools, unfortunately, an appreciation of these fundamental dynamics is absent—indeed, unimaginable. The fact that our understanding of ourselves and the world is not completely of our own making is a strange concept in most U.S. schools at the end of the twentieth century. A critical hermeneutics aware of such political and pedagogical concepts will facilitate the work of those dedicated to the construction of just schools that work to empower students regardless of their socioeconomic and cultural background. Our task is monumental, but our vision is powerful.

REFERENCES

Bellah, R., et al. (1991). *The good society.* New York: Vintage Books.

Block, F. (1990). *Postindustrial possibilities: A critique of economic discourse.* Berkeley: University of California Press.

Bottomore, T. (1984). *The Frankfurt School.* London: Tavistock.

Brosio, R. (1985). A bibliographic essay on the world of work. Paper presented to the American Educational Studies Association, Chicago. November.

Brosio, R. (1994). *The radical democratic critique of capitalist education.* New York: Peter Lang.

Chesneaux, J. (1992). *Brave modern world: The prospects for survival.* New York: Thames & Hudson.

Denzin, N., & Lincoln, Y. (1994). Introduction: Entering the field of qualitative research. In N. Denzin & Y. Lincoln (Eds.), *Handbook of qualitative research* (pp. 1–17). Thousand Oaks, CA: Sage.

Feinberg, W. (1989). Foundationalism and recent critiques of education. *Educational Theory, 39*(2), 133–138.

Gibson, R. (1984). *Structuralism and education.* London: Hodder & Stoughton.

Giroux, H. (1983). *Theory and resistance in education.* South Hadley, MA: Bergin & Garvey.

Giroux, H. (1997). *Pedagogy and the politics of hope: Theory, culture, and schooling.* Boulder, CO: Westview.

Greene, M. (1988). *The dialectic of freedom.* New York: Teachers College Press.

Greene, M. (1995). *Releasing the imagination: Essays on education, the arts, and social change.* San Francisco: Jossey-Bass.

Harvey, D. (1989). *The condition of postmodernitv.* Cambridge, MA: Basil Blackwell.

Held, D. (1980). *Introduction to critical theory: Horkheimer to Habermas.* Berkeley: University of California Press.

Home, D. (1986). *The public culture.* Dover, DE: Pluto Press.

Jay, M. (1973). *The dialectical imagination: A history of the Frankfurt School and the Institute of Social Research, 1923–1950.* Boston: Little, Brown.

Kellner, D. (1990). *Television and the crisis of democracy.* Boulder, CO: Westview.

Kincheloe, J., & McLaren, P. (1994). Rethinking critical theory and qualitative research. In N. Denzin & Y. Lincoln (Eds.), *Handbook of qualitative research* (pp. 138–157). Thousand Oaks, CA: Sage.

Lyotard, J. (1984). *The postmodern condition.* Minneapolis: University of Minnesota Press.

Macedo, D. (1994). *Literacies of power: What Americans are not allowed to know.* Boulder, CO: Westview.

McLaren, P. (1994). *Life in schools: An introduction to critical pedagogy in the foundations of education.* White Plains, NY: Longman.

McLaren, P., Hammer, R., Reilly, S., & Sholle, D. (1995). *Rethinking media literacy: A critical pedagogy of representation.* New York: Peter Lang.

Scholes, R. (1982). *Semiotics and interpretation.* New Haven: Yale University Press.

Shor, I. (1992). *Empowering education: Critical teaching for social change.* Chicago: University of Chicago Press.

Smart, B. (1992). *Modern conditions, postmodern controversies.* New York: Routledge.

Steinberg, S. (1998). *Ain't we "misbehavin"? White males in film.* New York: Peter Lang.

Steinberg, S., & Kincheloe, J. (1997). (Eds.). *Kinderculture: Corporate constructions of childhood.* Boulder, CO: Westview.

Toward a Curriculum of Mythopoetic Meaning

KATHLEEN R. KESSON

OUR GROUP OF CURRICULUM LEADERS is meeting for the third time in the anteroom of the Bellwether School, a small alternative school in Williston. Large snowflakes drift outside the visual frame of the windows as a late winter storm moves through this part of central Vermont. We are a small group today, due perhaps to the weather, perhaps to the extraordinary demands on the time of our group members. Against the backdrop of children's excited voices as they depart for the day, we struggle to find a way to enter into this discussion of mythopoesis (Gr. *muthos,* story + *poiein,* to make) and meaning. It is an awkward beginning. The mythopoetic genre of curriculum theorizing encompasses a broad range of intertwined perspectives: narrative and autobiography, psychoanalysis, aesthetics, and spirituality. It speaks to what is perhaps most basic in human beings—the capacities to feel, to empathize, to imagine, and to reflect on the larger purposes and meanings of our lives. It is about the *tacit,* rather than the *explicit,* layers of experience. It is about the *immeasurables* in educational theory and practice, and indeed it is perhaps this quality of immeasurability that has led to its neglect in the discourses of schooling.

We dance around the ideas expressed in the first draft of the essay, and Sarah attempts to articulate her lack of responsiveness, not to the ideas in the paper, which she considers "essential" to any discussion of curriculum, but to the somewhat disembodied form in which they initially were presented. She reminds me that the "medium is the message," and we begin to grasp at ways to enter into a dialogue about the somewhat elusive ideas presented in this chapter. We opt for storytelling as

Understanding Democratic Curriculum Leadership. Copyright © 1999 by Teachers College, Columbia University. All rights reserved. ISBN 0-8077-3826-3 (pbk), ISBN 0-8077-3827-1 (cloth). Prior to photocopying items for classroom use, please contact the Copyright Clearance Center, Customer Service, 222 Rosewood Dr., Danvers, MA 01923, USA, tel. (508) 750-8400.

perhaps the most compelling entry into the intangibility of the mythopoetic dimensions of curriculum. Nancy, who is now a curriculum coordinator for a large school district, tells us a story that hearkens back to her early days of teaching:

> It must have been my second year of teaching high school English in Massachusetts. I was new in the school, so of course they gave me all the really hard kids. I was trying everything I could think of to get the kids to write. Well, I decided—this must have been one of John's ideas [John, her husband, is an education professor]— that we would go on a little astral excursion. (Laughter). So, I turned off the lights, we took off our shoes, we sat on the floor, I probably lit a candle, and we started to take our astral journey. . . . And the assistant principal, who was a former marine sergeant, chose that moment to observe my classroom. . . . And he was a mean son of a gun, and I was really scared of him—he was real mean to the kids. . . . And he opened the door, and looked around and shut the door really quickly. And the kids . . . I immediately turned on the lights . . . and the kids said, "Boy, are you in trouble!"

We have a good laugh, and ask Nancy about the ending of this story. "Well," she said, "I didn't get fired. He didn't talk to me about it. But I *knew* that—or at least I *thought* that—I *could* get in trouble."

Educators often assert confidently that it doesn't really matter what is written explicitly in curriculum documents or district policies—the truth being that when teachers close their doors, they go ahead and do what they wish anyway. In this story, Nancy closed her door and attempted to do what, in her professional judgment, might facilitate the kind of learning that she was hoping for in her students—and horror of horrors, the usually invisible hand of curriculum authority suddenly became the visible presence of her immediate supervisor. It is something that many teachers consciously or unconsciously dread—getting "caught in the act" of transgressing the boundaries of the curriculum. But what exactly *are* the boundaries of the curriculum, and what constituted "out-of-bounds" in this story?

Nancy was having trouble motivating these hard-to-reach students and getting them to engage with ideas of significance. She intuitively understood that she needed to initiate a process by which they might become more connected to a sense of genuine personal meaning. Clearly, she felt that establishing an atmosphere of interpersonal trust was necessary for the journey to intrapersonal awareness (Gardner, 1983). To do this, she felt it necessary to alter the usual environment of the classroom, establishing a level of comfort (taking off shoes), equality (all sitting on the floor), introspection (turning off the light), and focus (lighting a candle). To the assistant principal, this "altered state" must have resembled a seance, or a meditation circle!

Indeed, an "astral journey" signifies a shift of attention from the "out there" of the explicit curriculum, to the "in here" of personal consciousness. To shamans, mystics, artists, poets, dreamers, and so-called "primitive people" (people who still live in intimate connection with the land and who do not participate in modern industrial society), the astral realm is a psychic zone of mystery, magic, myth, ancestors, and wandering spirits. In modern psychoanalytical terms, it is that domain of the unconscious from which we modern Western people have become effectively split. To many modern people, it is a chaotic and dangerous region inhabited by sensation, emotion, image, imagination, dream, fantasy, intuition, desire, passion, and the creative spirit—not the stuff of pure reason, logical analysis, or the public school curriculum! Nancy and her students were co-conspirators in this transgression, and they all clearly understood that some boundary had been crossed, indicated by their collective response when the authority figure unexpectedly came upon them.

How did it come to be that such an important aspect of human experience, indeed one that had been a central focus of human attention for millennia, has become *taboo* territory? What is it we fear about these "hidden" dimensions of the human mind? What is lost when we accede to this "splitting off" of entire layers of experience? And why, as one of the curriculum leaders in our group asked, "is all the important stuff so controversial"?

THE MODERN MIND

The analysis and critique of "modernity" has become a central focus of some curriculum theorists, as well as of philosophers and social theorists outside the field of education. Modernity can be understood in many different ways, depending on which historical framework one consults. For our purposes I will use the term "modernity" to talk about a way of life that has been shaped by the advent of scientific thinking, the growth of technology, the development of reason as a way of comprehending the world, and the increasing secularization of the world (Nietzsche called this last trend "the death of the gods"). Modernity has been characterized by the expansion of principles such as individual human rights, the nation-state, the ownership of property, the free market, the "social contract," and "Man's" dominion over nature. In modernity, humans supposedly have overcome their earlier reliance on myth, magic, and superstition as organizing principles, as well as their "embeddedness" in nature. The world, as historian Morris Berman (1981) and others have pointed out, has become "disenchanted." We have become fully conscious human beings (the story goes), employing reason, logic, empiricism, and abstract thinking to gain power and control over the forces of nature.

However, many theorists now speak about the multiple and interlocking "crises of modernity." Environmental critics express concern for the damage to our natural world wrought by the purely technical and instrumental applications of scientific thought and invention. Feminist critics decry the patriarchal paradigm that has devalued emotion, sensuality, and intuition in favor of cold logic. Indigenous people and their supporters have challenged the racist, colonialist mentality that has conquered, subordinated, and exploited "nonmodern" people all over the planet, and destroyed their cultures, land, livelihood, and languages. Social theorists note the cultural fragmentation, loss of community, and social alienation common to the people of modern, capitalist, industrial cultures. Religious leaders talk about the "crisis of faith." Even without the discourses of theorists to inform us about these interlocking crises, our everyday awareness of the problems of violence, poverty, war, economic instability, alienation, and environmental damage inform us all that there is something deeply amiss in modern culture. For teachers, the crises are painfully evident in the lives of many of our students.

Many theorists agree that there is an important epistemological basis for the more explicit social and ecological crises. They have suggested that *the very way we think* is implicated in the development of these many interrelated problems (Bohm, 1980; Capra, 1982; Griffin, 1988). Not only has the emphasis on calculating reason and analytical thinking, combined with a purely materialist, mechanistic, and reductionist perspective, brought about these multiple and interlocking crises—the mind set represented by these epistemologies is incapable of healing these problems. We literally have *thought ourselves into* these problems, and, it is suggested, we may not be able to *think ourselves out* of them! What is necessary are new epistemologies, new ways of thinking, fresh forms of perception. Because *the way we think* is to a great extent the product of *the way we are educated*, it is important for curriculum leaders not only to understand the critique of modernity and the modern mind, but to acquaint ourselves with the discourses that present alternatives to these dominant epistemologies. The curriculum discourses signified by the term "mythopoetics" have become home to a wide range of ideas embracing the inquiry processes and curriculum practices that confront the dominant rationalist paradigm. I will touch on a few of them in this chapter and address some of the dilemmas that teachers and curriculum leaders face when they attempt to incorporate this rich body of theorizing into their practice.

MYTHOPOETICS AND THE FIELD OF CURRICULUM

The idea of curriculum as organized bodies of knowledge, and of formal learning as an instrumental means to predetermined ends, is a relatively recent phenomenon. For much of human history, people learned much of what they needed to know by imitating adults around them, through apprenticeships, through observing nature, through the sharing of stories, and through communal rituals that encoded the values and expected behaviors of the culture. In many cultures, dreams and visions constituted an important component of this informal curriculum. This "unseen world" played a significant part in the everyday affairs of people, and "reality" was a multidimensional, interpenetrating network of experiences. Things have changed radically in modern industrialized cultures; the curricular emphasis is on abstract, explicit, and decontextualized knowledge, and schooling is systematized, routinized, and for the most part standardized.

Curriculum, as a field of study, has concerned itself for much of the twentieth century with such practical, external realities as discipline-specific knowledge, behavioral objectives, lesson planning, evaluation, classroom organization and management, learning theory, institutional structures, and how all of these elements intersect. The early days of curriculum theory took place in a social atmosphere in which an emerging professional class believed in the possibilities of "social engineering"; that is, in the possibility of controlling major aspects of the culture through careful scientific planning. Thus, there were efforts to make the field of curriculum "scientific," resulting in technical, managerial approaches to the problems of schooling. Technical approaches emphasized procedures over ethical decision making, while managerial approaches attempted to "teacher-proof" the curriculum with externally prescribed content and instructional practices, often developed by university "experts." It was both tacitly and explicitly assumed that the aim of education was to develop increasingly abstract thought and objective rationality. Although they received significant attention during the brief heyday of progressive education in the 1930s, aspects of education such as manual training, practical, experiential learning, and the kinds of affective and sensuous experiences embodied by the arts were (and still are, to a large extent) on the lower rungs of the knowledge hierarchy.

It was not until the late 1960s, with that decade's explosion of interest in human potential, consciousness research, and social change, that the field of curriculum was opened up to the exploration of the more subtle and mysterious dimensions of human experience signified by mythopoetics. A few curriculum theorists, working in relative isolation, challenged the predominant "scientism" of the curriculum field and began to look to the humanities for a new paradigm for understanding curriculum. Louise Berman was one of the first curriculum theorists to begin to draw upon humanistic and transpersonal psychologies, as well as existentialism, to challenge the overtly technical approaches to curriculum practice. In 1968, she wrote:

> Our hypothesis is that as the school places priority upon developing a setting where children and youth have the opportunity to experience and verbalize the meanings of creating, loving, knowing, organizing, and other process skills, they will orchestrate more beautifully the components of tomorrow's world than if they did not have such new priorities established in the curriculum. (quoted in Pinar, Reynolds, Slattery, & Taubman, 1995, p. 174)

These "new priorities" in the curriculum, reflected in the emergent concern for the uniqueness of the individual, the construction of values, the location of meaning in experience, and a strong sense of justice and equality, found perhaps their greatest expression in the work of James Macdonald. Macdonald became a leading critic of the dehumanization of the modern world, the objectification of students in schools, the limitations of the "structures of the disciplines" approach to curriculum, and curricular and social engineering. In the mid-1970s, in a paper on the various ideologies of education, he introduced a notion that he called the "transcendental developmental ideology" of education (Macdonald, 1995). This perspective not only challenged older ideologies of education (including the "transmission" model, the Romantic, or child-centered, model, and the Progressive model), but also would correct what he thought to be the limiting, materialist focus of the radical or political view of education, which he considered a "hierarchical historical point of view that has outlived its usefulness both in terms of the emerging structure of the environment and of the psyches of people today" (p. 73). The transcendental developmental ideology would embrace progressive and radical values, according to Macdonald, but would be rooted in a deep spiritual awareness (drawing on the work of M. C. Richards, he used the term "centering"). Macdonald termed his methodology of development a "dual dialectic," a praxis involving reflective transaction between the individual ego and the inward subjective depths of the self, as well as between the individual ego and the outer objective structures of the environment. This method grew out of his critique of existing developmental theories (see Kohlberg & Mayer, 1972), which he thought neglected one or the other aspect of this praxis, thus failing to take into account the full dimensions of human "being."

Macdonald's ideas, coming as they did on the heels of the "consciousness revolution," helped to open the field of curriculum studies to an eclectic array of theoretical perspectives: humanistic, gestalt, and transpersonal psychologies; existentialism, phenomenology, holism and organicism in philosophy; literature; aesthetics; theology and mystical thought; and, recently, postmodernism. These perspectives found a home with the group of curriculum theorists called the Reconceptualists (a movement that began in the early 1970s), who are critical of the narrow "means/ends" understanding of curriculum exemplified by the Tyler rationale,[1] and who share a leftist political orientation concerned with issues of equality and identity. There has been a shift in the field away from curriculum design, development, and the control of learning toward the *understanding* of the many complex aspects of curriculum and schooling, an understanding that has been informed by the eclectic array of disciplinary perspectives noted above.

While there is general agreement that the academic field of curriculum has now been successfully "reconceptualized," the work of these scholars has had minor impact on the actual practice of curriculum development, design, and change. In many ways, curriculum practice in schools is still deeply embedded in older, behaviorist models that call for clearly defined objectives, carefully organized subject matter, and evaluations based on externally observed, measurable behaviors. It is almost as though over 30 years of sophisticated curriculum theorizing had taken place in a vacuum that excluded schools. William Pinar, one of the leaders of the Reconceptualists, and his colleagues have suggested that if there is a "second wave" of reconceptualization, elementary and secondary schools may well be the site of such a wave (Pinar et al., 1995, p. 39). How might such a "second wave" take form in the actual life of schools? This is perhaps the central question for curriculum practitioners who feel drawn to the discourse field of mythopoetics.

In terms of the implementation of practices suggested by the mythopoetic perspective, we can look to the practical field of holistic education, which began to emerge almost as a "grass-roots" movement parallel to the theoretical developments in the field of curriculum, and more or less independent of them (Miller, 1990). Holistic education emphasizes curriculum and instructional practices that address the "whole child"—body, mind, emotion, and spirit. In the early days of its emergence (1970s), holistic educational practices drew heavily on both the new brain research (some books, for example, devoted themselves to right brain/left brain theory) and the fields of humanistic and transpersonal psychology. The pedagogical emphasis was on the *processes* of learning, in contrast to the *content* of the curriculum, and on self-esteem, aesthetics, interpersonal dynamics, peak experiences, and, in some classrooms, meditation and other quasi-spiritual practices. In recent years, holistic education has taken a more critical turn and has begun to come to terms with the social, as opposed to the purely psychological, aspects of education. This concern for the social dimension of experience, and related issues such as racism, social justice, and environmental politics, is reflected in the recent change in the name of holistic education's primary academic journal, *Holistic Education Review*, to *Encounter: Education for Meaning and Social Justice*.

Despite its growing social concerns, holistic education has received about as much attention as mythopoetic curriculum theory in mainstream schooling! The study of human "being," in all of its complexity, and the application of these ideas to practice have proven to be incredibly controversial, as new understandings about human possibilities come into conflict with established beliefs and dogmas about human "nature." Much of the resistance to these new ideas about human potential comes from conservative religious groups, who are threatened by ideas that challenge historical doctrines. We will return to the difficult politics of a "curriculum of meaning" in the final pages of this chapter. First, let's touch upon some of the central components of a mythopoetic curriculum theory and practice.

STORIES AND THE MYTHOPOETIC IMAGINATION

In *Dewey and Eros: Wisdom and Desire in the Art of Teaching,* Jim Garrison (1997) speaks of the centrality of stories in defining our lives: "Individual human existence is an event best recognized by its narrative structure. It has a beginning, a middle, and an end; a plot line; characters; a setting; and moments of active disclosure" (p. 45). For all of the human history that we know of, we have made stories to tell ourselves—stories of our origins, our purposes, our struggles, and our passions—and for centuries these stories have been "the curriculum." Stories have encoded the information, gathered over millennia of lived experience, that is necessary for survival in particular bio-regions (the Australian Aboriginal "Dreamtime" narratives are powerful living examples of this). Stories have transmitted values and ethics that bind communities together. With their explication of consequences for actions, they have facilitated the development of culturally specific norms of behavior. And, perhaps most important, they have attempted to explain, order, and attribute meaning to phenomena in what otherwise might appear to be a random and chaotic world. Indeed, the evolution of our cosmology (the story of our origins and our place in the universe) is simply the triumph of one story over another.

Stories are so pervasive throughout the world and throughout history that one might assume, as does curriculum theorist Kieran Egan (1989), that our brains are somehow "hard-wired" to respond to the narrative form. Psychoanalytical theory supports this idea. From a Freudian perspective, Bruno Bettleheim, in *The Uses of Enchantment* (1976), details the ways in which a child's engagement with the characters in fairy tales facilitates the resolution of fundamental early conflicts such as the Oedipal complex. The psychoanalyst C. G. Jung, with his extensive research into the unconscious mind, acknowledged that the archetypes and symbolic images in stories, myths, and dreams correspond to important psychological processes inherent in the adult individuation process as well. Jean Piaget, the cognitive psychologist, essentially agreed with Jung, although he understood the archetypes to be by-products of cognitive structures, rather than directly inherited from the biologically based, collective unconscious proposed by Jung. According to consciousness researcher Ken Wilber (1995), whether we agree with Freud, Jung, or Piaget, "the conclusion is essentially the same: all the world's great mythologies exist today in each of us, in me and in you. They are produced, and can at any time be produced, by the archaic, the magic, and the mythic structures of our own compound individuality" (p. 220).

Certainly, the popularity of books such as Clarissa Estés' *Women Who Run with the Wolves* (1992), and the contemporary psychoanalytical interest in stories, suggest such a symbiotic relationship between stories, our mythic past, and our psyches. For many people, the interior imagery of such stories provides a bridge to the less accessible aspects of consciousness, providing them with "raw material" for spiritual and psychological growth and development.

The "mythopoetic imagination," when carefully cultivated, is a rich and fertile field of images and archetypes. These symbols are the "ground" of deeply embedded metaphors that themselves shape the stories that are possible to tell. As language theorists have pointed out, our metaphors literally construct the world and our responses to it. The myth of Pandora's box, for example, metaphorically provides a potent psychological inhibitor when we are considering unleashing forces that may get out of our control! The mythopoetic, then, encompasses not only the realm of narrative, but the very architecture and language of the self—the many and complex layers of the human psyche, including what we consider to be the spiritual dimensions of experience. One important approach to this "archaeology of the self" is the practice of autobiography, or personal narrative.

AUTOBIOGRAPHY AND PERSONAL NARRATIVE

I regularly ask my college students, those who plan to be teachers and those who already are practicing educational professionals, "What significant aspects of life were left out of your education?" I have posed this question to various groups of students hundreds of times. People invariably answer in no uncertain terms: the emotional, the creative, the aesthetic, the *self*. It is tragic to think that so many people, teachers and students alike, are profoundly alienated by a system of education that literally leaves out the *self*!

Howard Gardner's (1983) work on "personal intelligences" has alerted many educators to the importance of the intra- and interpersonal dimensions of cognition. In a videotaped presentation of his ideas, Gardner, when asked what he thought was the most important intelligence, stated that the intrapersonal, with its emphasis on deep self-knowledge, was clearly the intelligence of primary importance for a successful adult life! His categorizing of these aspects of experience as "intelligences," as well as the more recent popular work on "emotional intelligence" by Daniel Goleman (1995) and others, hopefully will foster the inclusion of the self in the school curriculum. In Vermont, personal development is one of the primary categories for curriculum development. The *Framework* asks that teachers focus on such aspects of development as healthy choices, goal setting, decision making, personal economics, relationships, and careers, mostly explicit categories rather than the kind of deep search for meaning suggested by a mythopoetic focus. The inclusion of the self in the curriculum, and the search for meaning, are mostly evident in aspects of whole language programs such as journal writing and reader response logs, in which students express the personal meaning they gain from reading texts. Little progress has been made toward the radical reorganization of the curriculum around the deeply felt needs and interests of students, although that is certainly what this move in curriculum theory might suggest.

One of the more fruitful lines of development in curriculum inquiry, and one that relates most profoundly to the absence of the self in curriculum thought, is the genre of autobiographical research. Connelly and

Clandinin (1988) state that the best way to study curriculum is to study our "personal knowledge" (p. 4). The establishment of autobiography as an important curriculum discourse owes its success largely to the work of William Pinar and Madeline Grumet, with the publications of "Currere: Toward Reconceptualization" (Pinar, 1975) and *Toward a Poor Curriculum* (Pinar & Grumet, 1976). This genre of curriculum theory locates curricular meaning in the lived experience of the individual, rather than in the abstractions of subject matter. According to Pinar and colleagues (1995), the field of curriculum, with its preoccupation with "the public and the visible, with design, sequencing, implementation, evaluation, and in its preoccupation with curricular materials, . . . ignored the individual's experience of those materials" (p. 519).

Curriculum theorists since the time of the early Progressive Education movement have tried to locate the source of curriculum integration in the consciousness of the student (the self/knowledge connection), yet the current interest in curriculum integration still is concerned primarily with the linkages between subjects (as in the "Fields of Knowledge" of the Vermont *Framework*). Perhaps Gardner's theory of personal intelligences, Goleman's work on emotional intelligence, and the work of autobiographical curriculum theorists will help us realize the centrality of the self in the making of meaning.

Autobiography, as method of inquiry, seeks to overcome the profound alienation of schooling and estrangement from the self that constitute the educational experience of many students *and* teachers. It provides a method for the systematic search of our inner experience. Drawing on phenomenological, existential, and psychoanalytical sources of inquiry, one's "lived experience" becomes a source of data for understanding curricular issues. Utilizing our lived experience in curriculum discussions moves the center of discourse away from how to implement external mandates to an effort to understand the real effects of policies on the lives of teachers and students. It forces us to ask the educational questions that should be at the core of our debates, but that too often are forgotten: What is worth knowing? What do we value? How should we live our lives? What is transient and what is timeless? What kind of world do we want to create? As one curriculum leader in our group said, "I just want somebody to ask different kinds of questions."

Autobiographical work sometimes has been misunderstood as "asocial," but scholars, such as Janet Miller (1992), emphasize the collaborative and social character of such research. The method, says Miller, "attempts to bring teachers' voices to the center of the dialogue and debate surrounding current educational reform, teacher education restructuring efforts, and research on teachers' knowledge" (in Pinar et al., 1995,

p. 524). In this sense, it is potentially a politically potent move that confronts the bureaucratized decision-making apparatus of the educational "system."

SPIRITUALITY AND THE CURRICULUM

Long a taboo topic in educational circles, spirituality recently has become a "hot topic" in educational theory. Over the past few years, I have participated in a number of seminars and symposia devoted to the issue of spirituality and education, or spirituality and curriculum, at the annual meetings of the American Educational Research Association, the American Educational Studies Association, and the Journal of Curriculum Theory Conference. Inevitably, the conversations center around a desire for definition: What is spirituality? Is it different from religion? Does spirituality require belief in a Creator? Once the difficulties of discourse are acknowledged, the conversations usually branch from these unresolved questions of definition into discussions about the difficulty of finding common ground from which to teach ethics and morality, the importance of teaching about religions in a way that fosters tolerance and respect, or the necessity of creating caring communities in schools. The dominant concern of liberal educators is the preservation of the boundaries between church and state, an important and interesting postmodern dilemma, which, however, abdicates responsibility for a serious rethinking of curriculum in terms of what we are coming to understand about spiritual development. One of the most cogent articulations of spiritual development as it relates to the processes of education can be found in James Moffett's book *The Universal Schoolhouse: Spiritual Awakening Through Education* (1994).

What has been clear to me in these forums, and in other public forums, is that despite the great scientific and technological advances of the twentieth century, many modern people are increasingly disenchanted with lives focused on material success, the acquisition of consumer goods, and the search for status, security, and power. More and more people are turning to contemplative practices and spiritual disciplines to fill the void of meaning in modern life. A veritable explosion of books, seminars, and courses on spiritual development suggests that as a culture we are in a period of spiritual revitalization and renewal. And yet, the rhetoric of schooling and school reform suggests that economic competition, the drive for material success, and the search for status, security, and power are the only things that matter.

In curriculum theory, a genre of study called "curriculum as theological text" has emerged to address issues of spirituality. The focus of much of the writing in this genre seeks to reclaim the moral, ethical, and prophetic voices usually associated with religious scholarship in order to amplify the understanding of curriculum as a profoundly moral and spiritual endeavor. David Purpel's book *The Moral and Spiritual Crisis in Education* (1989) is a fine example of this type of scholarship. Nel Noddings's (1989) work on feminist theory and theology, Donald Oliver and Kathleen Gershman's (1989) work on cosmology, Doug Sloan's (1983) work on insight and imagination, and Pat Slattery's (1992) work on eschatology all contribute important dimensions to this thinking. Theorists who work in this genre understand education as "wedded to the most profound issues of the human heart and soul," and are concerned with "those mystical yearnings for union with the source of life, the nature of morality in an evil world, and those mythico-imaginative longings of the human spirit" (Pinar et al., 1995, p. 659).

"Schooling," says Nancy, one of the curriculum leaders in our group, "is a religious function divorced from spiritual layers of meaning." Indeed, schools are laden with rituals and initiations. Football games, bonfires, exams, pledging allegiance to the flag, and graduation ceremonies all evoke archaic ritual forms of the past. But these ritual forms are mostly devoid of anything but secular meaning—they do not, as rituals have done for centuries, connect the everyday with the sacred, the known with the unknown, the visible with the invisible, or human beings with the great mysteries of life. The price of this loss is high. Contemporary African ritual theorist Malidoma Some (1995) reminds us of this, with his compelling critique of modern "disenchanted" culture: "Where ritual is absent, the young ones are restless or violent, there are no real elders, and the grown-ups are bewildered. The future is dim" (p. 28).

"There is a very real message," Nancy continues, "that we in general send to kids through schooling, and that is that they need to be something that they aren't yet, and this is a profoundly anti-spiritual message!" She went on to tell how she came to this realization through her recent experience caring for someone who was dying. Looking for help in dealing with all of the profound issues that come up in such a situation, she went to a "spiritual master of sorts," and asked: "How can I understand this? How can I go with her as far as I can go without going all the way? How can I help her? How can I . . . grok [a term from Robert Heinlein's science fiction classic, *Stranger in a Strange Land*, meaning to deeply feel and understand] the magic of this?" The spiritual teacher reminded her that she was looking outside of herself for things she already knew. For Nancy, this was a moment of illumination, in which she came to understand the falsity of the premise that underpins much of our thinking about school-

ing: that is, the notion that students, as they are, are "not good enough
. . . they are unfinished products, and that we must 'fix' them." We won-
dered what education might be like if we could rid ourselves of this false
"deficit premise" and begin to attend to the knowledge and strengths and
creative insights that students bring to the learning process!

Our discussion group agrees that there are many more dimensions
to the human experience than what is addressed in schools. We agree
that this neglect is responsible for much of the alienation and anomie that
we find in schools. We discuss the irony in the fact that while books like
the *Celestine Prophecy* are mass market phenomena, and as one teacher
said, "the students are doing Tarot readings in the halls," a serious and
sustained academic discussion of these issues is "out-of-bounds" in the
school curriculum! "There are these things going on in the culture . . .
how do kids learn to have a conversation about them? . . . Isn't it about
'cultural literacy'? . . . How can we educate them to think about these
issues?" Some of our members express a concern that few teachers whom
they know are equipped to deal in a sophisticated way with these topics.
As one curriculum leader pointed out, "Spiritual understandings, including morality, usually develop within a particular religious context—few
people know how to address these issues from a comparative perspective." Many teachers do consider the spiritual dimension important in
their own personal lives, but find few bridges for these understandings
into their professional lives. The discussion of spiritual development, and
of related social and philosophical issues, is clearly a direction for professional development if we take seriously the task of educating students in
a way that both supports their own spiritual development and enables
them to live successfully in a religiously pluralistic new society.

One of the group members brought up the politics here in Vermont
around the inclusion of the word *spirituality* in the new *Framework.* Many
of us were surprised to find at one point in the development of the *Framework* that spirituality was, in fact, included under the section on personal
development, as part of a definition of the development of the "whole
person" (including the emotional, physical, intellectual, and spiritual dimensions). We watched with interest how the word would disappear and
reappear in subsequent versions of the document. Finally, it was gone for
good, along with all references to ethics and values. The story of the inclusion in and exclusion from the *Framework* of spirituality, ethics, and values indicates the intense controversy around these ideas and highlights
the political nature of curriculum policy making. Certain groups in the
state had raised objections about the very presence of "social responsibility" and "personal development" in the *Framework,* even though these
were two out of the four categories that emerged from the grass-roots

deliberation process. Their influence clearly was felt at the level of the State Board, and a recommendation had been made to scratch these aspects from the *Framework*. The question became whether people wanted to risk losing these two "Vital Results" altogether by the presence of "trigger words" such as spirituality and ethics. The decision was made to compromise by removing the troublesome words. One of our curriculum leaders notes that while the word is absent from the state *Framework,* her district has chosen to include it in their district framework. This is a good example of the kind of local autonomy that is still cherished in Vermont.

The fear, of course, about including spirituality in the curriculum is the fear that the delicate and fuzzy boundary between the Church and State will be crossed. The focus on this aspect, which is really about protecting people's religious beliefs from the incursions of government and not favoring one religion over another in public life, has prevented us from more sophisticated thinking about the topic. I think it is safe to say that few, if any, curriculum theorists believe that this boundary should be diminished in any way. Bringing in the mythopoetic dimension of experience is not about bringing a particular religious teaching into the schools; it's about a way of teaching that *fosters the making of personal meaning.* Of course, a curriculum that fosters personal meaning is a very real threat to externally imposed systems of meaning, which is why it remains controversial.

A spiritual approach to education is not so much about *what* should be taught but *how* we should teach. This raises the question, of course, of whether curriculum is "object" or "method." I believe that it broadens our thinking to include the notion of "method" in our curriculum deliberations, not in the sense of "technique," which is how method has come to be understood, but in the sense of *who one is* as a teacher, what parts of oneself are brought to the teaching and learning encounter. Teaching for meaning making requires that we see below the surface of our students into the subjective depths of their personality. It asks that we see our students in all their potential fullness of being, not as flawed parts on an academic assembly line. It asks us, as Macdonald (1995) suggests, to encounter the "indwelling spirit" of the people we teach. It asks us to be open and vulnerable ourselves in the presence of those we teach. It asks us to focus on the development of habits of mind that many consider central to a spiritual presence in the world: reverence, respect, awe, wonder, reflection, vision, commitment, and purpose. But how, in a concrete way, can we teach for the development of these subtle habits of mind? Let's turn now to the forms of representation most central to the act of meaning making, the arts.

FORMS OF REPRESENTATION OF THE MYTHOPOETIC

Taking into consideration the issues raised in the discussion of narrative, autobiography, and spirituality, one way we might now characterize mythopoesis is as *the profoundly personal lived experience of human beings, in all of its depth and complexity.* Such a rich and complex understanding of ourselves suggests the need for multiple and imaginative forms of expression. The arts offer a rich variety of expressive devices that enliven the mythopoetic dimension of the curriculum. Nelson Haggerson, in a conference presentation about the mythopoetic genre of curriculum studies, once listed poetry, stories, music, dance, sculpture, painting, movies (video), photographs, drama, letters, autobiography, rituals, architecture, and signs as essential forms of representation.

The arts affirm and reveal the unique individuality of our students. They provide rich opportunities for individual and collective meaning making. They provide a pluralistic approach to cognition and offer multiple entry points into concepts and ideas, and they can provoke students into newer, more complex understandings. Curriculum theorists and philosophers of education such as Elliot Eisner (1992), Kieran Egan (1992), Maxine Greene (1995), and Harry Broudy (1988) all argue persuasively that the cultivation of the intellect—the "capacity to generalize, analyze, and synthesize concepts" (Pinar et al., 1995, p. 569)—requires the cultivation of the imagination.

Aside from the importance of the arts to personal development, I want to argue for their importance to the democratic project upon which this book is based. Recent controversies over the funding of the arts indicate our high degree of ambivalence about the social function of the arts. The arts are indeed dangerous: While they certainly can be used to nurture tradition, they also can destabilize us and challenge the known and the given. They require us to look at everything in new ways, with fresh perspectives. They can be value laden, and communicate controversial points of view, thus opening up new and unexplored possibilities for social life. Art can foster the kind of independent thinking, the rich diversity of perspective that, while frightening to some, is crucial for the development of an interdependent democratic spirit. Maxine Greene (1995) talks about the ways in which the arts enable "a pluralism of vision" and "a multiplicity of realities." It is for all these reasons that art is both dangerous and necessary.

These ideas, compelling as I believe they are, do not seem to have found general acceptance in the education community or the general public, and the marginalization of the arts in the school curriculum says much to us about the contemporary importance of the mythopoetic in these settings. I am hopeful, after witnessing the incredible impact that the work of Howard Gardner (1993), with his theory of multiple intelligences, has had on educational decisions and the direction of policy in the State of Vermont, that the arts will come to be understood and valued to a greater extent than we have seen in the past. Teachers and curriculum leaders, however, will need more than a passing acquaintance with Gardner's cognitive theory if the arts are to become a significant component of the curriculum. A superficial understanding of the theory is likely to perpetuate the status of the arts as "add-ons" or "frills," nonessential to the core curriculum. On the other hand, a deep philosophical understanding of the centrality of the arts to human experience (Dewey, 1934) and an understanding of the various epistemologies (ways of knowing), cognitive processes, and meaning-making capacities of the various art forms might elevate the arts to their rightful status.

Aesthetic forms of knowing, while important to consider in terms of inclusion in the school curriculum, have another dimension of significance to curriculum theorists and curriculum leaders. The scholarship of Jose Rosario (1979), Elizabeth Vallance (1991), Elliot Eisner (1985), and Thomas Barone (1993), among others, has opened the field up to new frameworks by which curriculum leaders can come to understand curriculum issues. A genre of curriculum inquiry called "aesthetic inquiry" has emerged as a legitimate form of research in the field. Aesthetic inquiry draws on the methods of art critics as a way to understand, analyze, and critique what goes on in classrooms and learning institutions. Contrasting aesthetic inquiry with quantitative educational research, Elizabeth Vallance notes that "aesthetic inquiry has the same purposes as traditional experimental research: it seeks to help the researcher—and others—to see the qualities of a curriculum that help account for students' and educators' reactions to it" (Pinar et al., 1995, p. 573). Such "aesthetic knowing," carefully cultivated, could enrich and enliven curriculum deliberations.

CONCLUSION

The work of curriculum leaders occurs in complex political networks, which are underpinned by multiple subjectivities, disparate beliefs, and complex webs of meanings. People's visions of what schooling should be are intimately connected with their visions of what constitutes the good life, the viable society. These meanings and beliefs sometimes lie below the surface of consciousness, and it falls to educational leaders to make the tacit, taken-for-granted realities explicit, problematic. It is an uneasy position to be in. The public discourse on schooling, however, must engage at the level of values, beliefs, and meanings if we are ever to create lasting change, not just pendulum swings, in our educational institutions.

If many teachers feel, and I believe they do, that this dimension of experience is an important one, what are the internal and/or external restraints that inhibit its importance in classrooms and in public discourse? Numerous times throughout our conversations, our group members reference the political realities that bound their work as teachers and as curriculum leaders. Based on past experiences and tacit understandings about what is possible, they have well-developed "internal radar" about trigger issues. No one wants to be the object of public outcry, and indeed the life of one of our group members had been made incredibly difficult because of the clash between her deeply felt commitments and organized community pressure. They ask what I think is a crucial question: Are these self-imposed taboos?

The notion of self-imposed taboos is central to an understanding of how hegemonic culture works. (Hegemony suggests an ideological framework that operates almost invisibly through a vast array of cultural forms, as opposed to the more crass forms of social conditioning found, for example, in authoritarian countries.) The system of rewards and punishments, the sense of right and wrong, and cultural and social norms all operate below the threshold of consciousness. This "information" is distributed throughout the psychosocial network. Some people, of course, internalize the expectations better than others, and those who don't respond readily to the tacit conditioning are subjected to harsher, more explicit methods. Poor people, for example, who have no illusions about the mythopoetics of the American dream, tend to act in ways that elicit sharp reaction from the "powers-that-be," and prisons are one of America's top growth industries.

That our understandings of the world and what is possible operate below the surface of consciousness is, I believe, a powerful argument for the inclusion of the mythopoetic in the curriculum and in curriculum deliberations. The capacities to see below the surface and understand the ways in which our thinking has been shaped (the negative pole of the dialectic most cogently developed by critical theorists), and the positive capacities to imagine things otherwise, to construct alternative realities, to think aesthetically and compassionately, to entertain the unthinkable and to know the unknowable, are *transformative* capacities. They provide us with the vision and the passion to change the world. What kind of a world might we construct if citizens were invigorated, from their earliest educational lives, with such imaginative and visionary capacities? Would we still suffer from "self-imposed taboos"? Or would we have the confidence to manifest our dreams?

The group members also talk about the very real personal, as well as political, reservations that they have about the mythopoetic. In many ways, they say, some of the things that get brought up in a curriculum of meaning making might best be left undisturbed, under the surface. We sometimes avoid personal narratives, they suggest, because we "don't want to open the proverbial can of worms." Pain lurks below the surface, as do issues of loss, grief, abuse, and fear. How can we deal with these issues and not have it be therapy? What will I have to deal with in myself if this stuff comes up in my classroom? We shift from the deeply felt to the ironic as they then ask, How will I get through the grammar book? And, perhaps most relevant to our immediate context, what standard will it meet?

Although hints of the mythopoetic were indeed present at many stages of the Vermont *Framework* deliberations (for example, with the inclusion of spirituality and ethics), the section on personal development, in which these capacities might reasonably be located, now focuses almost solely on physical fitness, goal setting, rational decision making, teamwork, and career planning. The disappearance of the mythopoetic, and the dominance of these latter standards, are due, in large part, to the increasing presence of business leaders in the deliberations, as well as the self-imposed taboos of the policy makers.

Group members suggest that as an education community, we might be overreacting to small organized groups and neglecting what may be the general will. We return to the story that opened our dialogue and explore the notion of "permission." Nancy was frightened to carry out her "astral journey" with her students because she didn't think she had "permission." But she muses about how she might respond to such a situation today:

> What I think I can do now in classrooms is a lot different from
> what I thought I could do that first year of teaching. Now I know
> how hard it is for someone to lose their job! If that man had
> wanted to go and get me for that, he would have had a hard time.
> But I didn't know that then.

Nancy's many years of experience as a teacher and as a curriculum leader have helped to demystify the systems of control and eliminate her self-imposed taboos. This suggests the importance of "mentoring" young teachers, who may have strong ideals and commitments, but be filled with fears of job loss and community censure if they "step outside the bounds" of the explicit curriculum. We return to the notion of "permission" and note ironically that it took the sustained cognitive research work of Harvard theorist Howard Gardner to finally "permit" teachers to focus on the intrapersonal dimensions of experience.

One other caveat I want to make is to note the tendency for bureaucratized systems to "disenchant" even powerful mythopoetic ideas and practices. In some ways, this realm of experience might better remain a subversive discourse and practice, rather than risk the kind of reification and routinization that often happen to otherwise compelling ideas when they become systematized. An example here is the use of journal writing, which was originally a novel and powerful approach to the making of personal meaning, and which many students now hate and resist, having journaled their way from kindergarten through high school!

The curriculum discourses concerned with mythopoesis, spirituality, and the arts, while distinct from each other, share a concern with the making of meaning. They are rich and eloquent discourses and can inspire us with visions and possibilities of what education could be if it took the most profound human questions to heart. Surely, those of us who care about the lives of children are concerned with the difficulties many young people have finding meaning in a confusing world. Surely, we care about the alienation many of them suffer in schools that do not validate their emotions, their creativity, their *selves*. The "discourses of meaning" require us to face up to these concerns and to facilitate public conversations about what kind of educational processes and environments might support a greatly expanded understanding of human intelligence and potential.

NOTE

1. Ralph Tyler is perhaps one of the century's most influential curricularists. His framework (Tyler, 1949) for curriculum design was deeply rooted in the "behaviorist" paradigm and called for the selection and organization of objectives, content, and activities that could be easily evaluated. His framework is the most concise demonstration of a linear, rationally controlled, and easily measurable approach to curriculum practice.

REFERENCES

Barone, T. (1993). Acquiring a public voice: Curriculum specialists, critical storytelling, and educational reform. *JCT, 10*(1).

Berman, M. (1981). *The reenchantment of the world*. New York: Basic Books.

Bettelheim, B. (1976). *The uses of enchantment: The meaning and importance of fairy tales*. New York: Knopf.

Bohm, D. (1980). *Wholeness and the implicate order*. London: Ark Paperbacks.

Broudy, H. (1988). Aesthetics and the curriculum. In W. F. Pinar (Ed.), *Contemporary curriculum discourses* (pp. 332–342). Scottsdale, AZ: Gorsuch Scarisbrick.

Capra, F. (1982). *The turning point*. New York: Simon & Schuster.

Connelly, M., & Clandinin, J. (1988). *Teachers as curriculum planners: Narratives of experience*. New York: Teachers College Press.

Dewey, J. (1934). *Art as experience*. New York: Perigree Books.

Egan, K. (1989). *Teaching as storytelling: An alternative approach to teaching and curriculum in the elementary school*. Chicago: University of Chicago Press.

Egan, K. (1992). *Imagination in teaching and learning: The middle school years*. Chicago: University of Chicago Press.

Eisner, E. (1985). *The educational imagination: On the design and evaluation of school programs* (2nd ed.). New York: Macmillan.

Eisner, E. (1992, April). The misunderstood role of the arts in human development. *Phi Delta Kappan, 73*(8), 591–595.

Estés, C. (1992). *Women who run with the wolves*. New York: Ballantine Books.

Gardner, H. (1983). *Frames of mind: The theory of multiple intelligences*. New York: Basic Books.

Gardner, H. (1993). *Multiple intelligences: The theory in practice*. New York: Basic Books.

Garrison, J. (1997). *Dewey and Eros: Wisdom and desire in the art of teaching*. New York: Teachers College Press.

Goleman, D. (1995). *Emotional intelligence*. New York: Bantam Books.

Greene, M. (1995). *Releasing the imagination*. San Francisco: Jossey-Bass.

Griffin, D. (1988). *The reenchantment of science*. Albany: State University of New York Press.

Kohlberg, L., & Mayer, R. (1972, November). Development as the aim of education. *Harvard Educational Review, 42*(4), 449–496.

Macdonald, J. B. (1995). A transcendental developmental ideology of education. In B. J. Macdonald (Ed.), *Theory as a prayerful act* (pp. 69–98). New York: Peter Lang.

Miller, J. L. (1992). Teachers, autobiography, and curriculum: Critical and feminist perspectives. In S. Kessler & B. Swadner (Eds.), *Reconceptualizing the early childhood curriculum: Beginning the dialogue* (pp. 103–122). New York: Teachers College Press.

Miller, R. (1990). *What are schools for?* Brandon, VT: Holistic Education Press.

Moffett, J. (1994). *The universal schoolhouse: Spiritual awakening through education*. San Francisco: Jossey-Bass.

Noddings, N. (1989). *Women and evil*. Berkeley: University of California Press.

Oliver, D., with Gershman, K. (1989). *Education, modernity and fractured meaning: toward a process theory of teaching and learning*. Albany: State University of New York Press.

Pinar, W. F. (1975). Currere: Toward reconceptualization. In W. F. Pinar (Ed.), *Curriculum theorizing: The reconceptualists* (pp. 396–414). Berkeley: Mc-Cutchan.

Pinar, W. (1994). *Autobiography, politics, and sexuality.* New York: Peter Lang.

Pinar, W. F., & Grumet, M. R. (1976). *Toward a poor curriculum.* Dubuque, IA: Kendall/Hunt.

Pinar, W. F., Reynolds, W. M., Slattery, P., & Taubman, P. M. (1995). *Understanding curriculum: An introduction to the study of historical and contemporary curriculum discourses.* New York: Peter Lang.

Purpel, D. (1989). *The moral and spiritual crisis in education: A curriculum for justice and compassion in education.* South Hadley, MA: Bergin & Garvey.

Rosario, J. (1979). Aesthetics and the curriculum: Persistency, traditional modes, and a different perspective. *JCT, 1*(1), 136–154.

Slattery, P. (1992). Toward an eschatological curriculum theory. *JCT, 9*(3), 7–12.

Sloan, D. (1983). *Insight-imagination: The emancipation of thought and the modern world.* Westport, CT: Greenwood Press.

Some, M. (1995). *Ritual: Power, healing, and community.* OR: Swan/Raven.

Tyler, R. W. (1949). *Basic principles of curriculum and instruction.* Chicago: University of Chicago Press.

Vallance, E. (1991). Aesthetic inquiry: Art criticism. In E. Short (Ed.), *Forms of curriculum inquiry* (pp. 155–172). Albany: State University of New York Press.

Wilber, K. (1995). *Sex, ecology, and spirituality: The spirit of evolution.* Boston: Shambhala Publications.

Three Personal Reflections

JAMES G. HENDERSON, KATHLEEN R. KESSON, & KERRIN A. McCADDEN

THIS BOOK PROVIDES A MAP for understanding *democratic curriculum leadership*. This map begins with an overview of the philosophy, ethics, and activities of this multidimensional educational reform practice. Attention then turns to four curriculum study topics that provide critical insight into this transformative work: curriculum deliberation, reflexive systems, cultural criticism, and educational mythopoetics. *Curriculum deliberation* highlights the importance of participatory, open-minded problem solving, while *reflexive systems* foreground the need for institutional flexibility and narrative interplay. *Cultural criticism* focuses on the deep-seated sociopolitical issues associated with democratic transformations, and *educational mythopoetics* touches on the heart and soul—the vital spirit—of this reform work.

To repeat a point made in the opening chapter, this book has been organized to facilitate the "dialogical journey" of democratic curriculum leaders. Each critical study topic presents a "truth" about the holistic intent of this leadership approach. Each chapter in this text provides insight into, and a unique perspective on, the meaning of a *caring learning community*. This book is designed to facilitate continuous professional growth characterized as the *hermeneutic circle*—the continuous reflection on the details of practice in light of selected critical theorizing and, reciprocally, the continuous critique of the critical theorizing in light of practical experience. In essence, this text has been written to foster the hermeneutic understanding of democratic curriculum leadership. It is designed to en-

Understanding Democratic Curriculum Leadership. Copyright © 1999 by Teachers College, Columbia University. All rights reserved. ISBN 0-8077-3826-3 (pbk), ISBN 0-8077-3827-1 (cloth). Prior to photocopying items for classroom use, please contact the Copyright Clearance Center, Customer Service, 222 Rosewood Dr., Danvers, MA 01923, USA, tel. (508) 750-8400.

courage a cyclical *rhythm* between progressive educational activity and multidimensional critical reflection.

We end this book with three personal reflections on the meaning of this curriculum leadership work, composed by three of the book's contributors: the two co-editors, Jim Henderson and Kathleen Kesson, and a member of the Vermont study group, Kerrin McCadden. We feel that these personal reflections are a fitting conclusion to this text because the political work of Deweyan democracy is highly personal in nature. We also feel that the placement of Kerrin's reflection at the end of the chapter is an important symbolic statement. By concluding with a practitioner's voice, we are emphasizing the point that the day-to-day, politically demanding and stressful work of democratic curriculum reform takes place in public schools, not in the minds of curriculum theorists.

A POETIC INTRODUCTION

To set the tone for our personal reflections, we open with excerpts from "Song of Myself," one of the *Leaves of Grass* poems by the great American poet, Walt Whitman. In intimate and idiosyncratic but very human and generous terms, Whitman (1855/1992) celebrates *democracy as a way of life:*

I celebrate myself, and sing myself,
And what I assume you shall assume,
For every atom belonging to me as good belongs to you.
I loafe and invite my soul,
I lean and loafe at my ease observing a spear of summer grass. . . .

Whoever degrades another degrades me,
And whatever is done or said returns at last to me.
Through me the afflatus surging and surging, through me the current and
    index.
I speak the pass-word primeval, I give the sign of democracy,
By God! I will accept nothing which all cannot have their counterpart of on
    the same terms. . . .

Divine am I inside and out, and I make holy whatever I touch or am
    touch'd from,
The scent of these arm-pits aroma finer than prayer,
This head more than churches, bibles, and all the creeds. . . .

I have said that the soul is not more than the body,
And I have said that the body is not more than the soul,

And nothing, not God, is greater to one than one's self is,
And whoever walks a furlong without sympathy walks to his own funeral
    drest in his shroud, . . .
I hear and behold God in every object, yet understand God not in the least,
Nor do I understand who there can be more wonderful than myself.

Why should I wish to see God better than this day?
I see something of God each hour of the twenty-four, and each moment
    then,
In the faces of men and women I see God, and in my own face in the glass,
I find letters from God dropt in the street, and every one is sign'd by God's
    name,
And I leave them where they are, for I know that wheresoe'er I go,
Others will punctually come for ever and ever. (pp. 22–67)

It could be said, in the spirit of Walt Whitman's poem, that this book has been written for those who are moved by a sense of human sympathy and interdependence. *Democracy as a way of living* has its visionaries— teachers, parents, and other curriculum stakeholders who have faith that *all* citizens of a country can, with educational assistance, undertake a life of authentic inquiry in a context of dialogue with diverse others. This book is designed to encourage and support these visionaries.

JIM'S REFLECTIONS

I was introduced to the field of curriculum studies while working on my masters degree in the social foundations of education, and I was quite impressed with the openness and autonomy of curriculum studies. Cherryholmes (1988) nicely captures the intellectual spirit of curriculum scholarship:

Curriculum is not derivative, as are many subfields of education, from other academic or applied disciplines. For example, educational psychology has roots in psychology; social foundations of education, in history and sociology. . . . Curriculum deals with problems that are uniquely educational in much the same way that instruction has its own special tasks. But instruction is confronted with the concrete situation of classrooms, students, content, and teachers. The tasks facing curriculum are less immediately demanding. Such independence is rare. It is enviable, however, if one desires to chart one's course by picking and choosing among problems and orientations. (pp. 130–131)

Because of the creative latitude permitted curriculum scholars, I decided to focus my doctoral studies in this educational subfield. And as my career has progressed, I've been quite happy with my decision.

When I entered curriculum studies, the distancing of the field from positivist, structuralist, and management systems discourse-practices was becoming well established. I resonated with the "intertextual" understandings of curriculum that were beginning to emerge, and I was influenced by Giroux's (1992) concept of "bordercrossings" and Pinar, Reynolds, Slattery, and Taubman's (1995) view of curriculum as an "extraordinarily complicated conversation" (p. 848). However, I did feel that this curriculum scholarship was limited in that it did not sufficiently challenge the curriculum theory/practice "border." In Pinar and colleagues' (1995) terms, it did not sufficiently encourage a "conversation" between critical curriculum scholars and progressive educational practitioners.

In the fall of 1995, I began to think how a critical theory–progressive practice dialogue could be established. After working out the *hermeneutic* blueprint for this project, I asked Kathleen Kesson to join me in this undertaking. I knew that Kathleen was a committed, well-informed curriculum scholar who daily worked with a diverse group of progressive Vermont educators. She was well positioned to link contemporary curriculum theory with a Deweyan interpretation of progressive education. This book is the result of this 2-year theory/practice engagement, and Kathleen's personal reflection will provide more of the details of this undertaking. What began as *hermeneutics in theory* ended as *hermeneutics in practice,* and Kerrin's personal reflection nicely captures that transition.

I would like to highlight the interpretation of "curriculum" that guided this 2-year theory/practice interplay and that is embodied in this book. *Curriculum* is a Latin term, first used in university educational discourses in the European Middle Ages (Jackson, 1992), and can be translated literally as an educational "race course" (Marsh & Willis, 1995, p. 6). There are over 120 distinctive definitions of "curriculum" in the literature (Portelli, 1987); and Pinar and colleagues' (1995) discussion of curriculum as an "historical, political, racial, gendered, phenomenological, autobiographical, aesthetic, theological, and international . . . conversation" (pp. 847–848) is certainly one of the most sophisticated of these definitions. This book builds on that interpretation by integrating *critical conversation* with *progressive practice.* In effect, this book promotes a view of "curriculum practice" as a *set of interrelated, critically informed, and collaborative activities centered on teaching for democratic living.*

In the first chapter of their book, Pinar and colleagues (1995) proclaim the "death" of curriculum development (p. 6). This book resurrects curriculum development as a vital and centrally important activity in societies with democratic ideals. However, the message of this book is that this renewed curriculum development can lose its moral bearings without the compass of a critical hermeneutics. A sophisticated menu of emancipatory concerns must inform this reform work daily. This book has been designed to foster an ongoing dialogue between critical theory and transformative practice. The book invites democratic curriculum leaders to engage in a particular continuing education—one that deepens their understanding of the dynamics, the dialectics, and the merits of their change efforts. The message of this text is that "curriculum" is *both* critical conversation and political practice. One without the other would be a solitary dance signifying a retreat from the daily challenges of co-constructing a democratic civilization.

An experienced teacher in one of my graduate classes recently asked me why I felt so deeply about "democracy as a moral way of life." Her question caught me by surprise, not so much because I didn't have a ready explanation. After all, this book itself is a response to her query. No, I was taken aback because of the way she asked the question. She didn't want me to respond as a curriculum professor, but in a personal way—as one human being to another. She wanted to know, deep down, what motivated me to take on this challenging reform work? I answered her question as best I could, and I now repeat my response in more measured prose.

I really don't know why I feel so strongly that a democratic way of living is the "good life." Perhaps it's because of my father, who was a pilot during World War II fighting German fascism and Japanese militarism. Although he came home as a victorious soldier, his fight for democracy was far from over. He became a high school teacher, and I grew up hearing about his continuous battles with a rigid, dogmatic, and manipulative principal. Perhaps it's because of my mother, who became a music teacher, in part because she was advised that, despite her math and science abilities, girls don't become mathematicians or scientists. Perhaps it's because of my involvement in the Vietnam antiwar movement, which made me wonder why so many Americans (including my father) were willing to "fight" for democratic principles but were not willing to engage in an open-minded, democratic dialogue over the pros and cons of this military engagement. Why would people say, "America, love it or leave it?" Why would a society with democratic ideals continue the French imperialist legacy in Indochina? Or perhaps it's because of my involvement in the free school movement, particularly the Milwaukee Independent School (MIS), while working on my master's degree. At MIS, I experienced education as a multilayered personal, social, spiritual, and political affair.

Or perhaps it's because of a powerful aesthetic, transcendent moment in my life near Albuquerque, New Mexico. A group of teaching friends and I were driving from Milwaukee, Wisconsin, to Santa Barbara, California, to attend a national alternative school conference. We had stopped at a motel outside of Albuquerque, and I awoke just before dawn. I decided to walk out into the desert air to watch the sun rise over the mountains. Enveloped in the sweet, pungent smells of sage and other desert plants, I was transported out of myself in an explosion of love vividly expressed by LePage (1987): "The forests speak out, the oceans beckon, the sky calls us forth, the plants want to share their story, the mind of the universe is open to all of us, the planet wants to instruct" (p. 180). Coming out of that moment and in a state of tears, I realized that my deepest moral feelings were not bounded by the traditional Roman Catholic beliefs of my childhood but, instead, were grounded in a loving, compelling invitation to live a life of continuous, expansive growth—a life of continuous becoming—involving both self and other. And over the years, I have come to understand that invitation as a radically open, playful, pragmatic, dialogical, ecological, and critical journey of meaning making that incorporates the sacred and the profane, the poetic and the prosaic, the aesthetic and the mundane, the intuitive and the rational, the visionary and the practical, the personal and the political, and an ethic of care and an ethic of justice. It is this disciplined, multiliterate (Eisner, 1994), multitextual (Pinar et al., 1995) understanding of life's "educative" (Dewey, 1938/1963) dynamics that inspired the hermeneutic design of this book.

For all of the above personal reasons, I have come to view the American story as inspiring and frustratingly unfulfilled—as a glass that is both half full and half empty. On the positive side, there is a historical tradition that includes a Declaration of Independence, a Constitution, and a Bill of Rights. There is a victorious rebel general, George Washington, who chose to become a democratic "citizen" rather than a military dictator. And so much more, so many more fortuitous events in the American fight for "freedom"! As someone whose undergraduate major was history and who taught elementary and high school social studies, I studied and celebrated this heritage.

But there is a downside to this American heritage. There is a history of Native American genocide, slavery, and capitalist elitism, as well as persistent racism, sexism, and homophobia. Clearly, America's democratic work has only begun, and I believe that the challenges to the "freedoms" are becoming more subtle as we enter the twenty-first century. As a curriculum scholar, I am becoming increasingly convinced that the real "enemy" of democracy is not external individuals—the Adolph Hitlers or

Saddam Husseins of the world—but rather the unenlightened, ignorant dimensions of the human psyche. I feel that, ultimately, the state of a democratic union is dependent on the state of its citizens' souls.

In the span of history, Americans generally have stood *against* overt forms of oppression; but what do Americans stand *for*? Is American "freedom" ultimately about marketplace competition and relentless consumerism? Or is it about a deeper "pursuit of happiness"? And is material wealth a distraction or a support for this deeper pursuit? How many Americans who have achieved a certain standard of living are willing to live a life of authentic inquiry? How many of them are willing to cultivate the sacredness of their own existence? Moore (1996) writes about our deepest enchantments and our many ways of love. He feels that if too many of us lose our sense of soul, "civil chaos is bound to ensue" (Moore, 1996, p.19). I share his concern as I continue to work for a deepening of the democratic ideals of my society through day-to-day educational reform activities.

KATHLEEN'S REFLECTIONS

I came to the field of curriculum studies in much the same way as Jim did, having been introduced to it during study for my master's degree in education, and later during my doctoral work. I had been a teacher, performing artist, education activist, community organizer, and, I might add, mother of four for a number of years before I attended graduate school. My life was essentially a life of practice, thoroughly involved with teaching, parenting, and community activism around a number of issues ranging from environmental politics, to peace and justice work, to education advocacy.

It was my engagement with politics, and the community education work I did around that, that awakened me to the mismatch between what I had learned in school in the 1950s and 1960s and what I found to be going on in the world. Why had I not heard anything about the Civil Rights Movement in my White suburban school? Why were we not taught about the dangers of nuclear war? Why had my history classes never studied anything from any angle other than the conqueror? Why had I despised high school, suffering endless hours of boredom? Along with this experiential awakening, I reveled in the writing of the "education radicals" of the 1960s and 1970s: Joel Spring, John Holt, Herb Kohl, Ivan Illich, Jonathan Kozol. Their books, which revealed the disheartening relationships between the organization of our capitalist economy and the organization and purposes of our schools, nurtured my critical consciousness and helped me to understand my somewhat instinctual resistance to bureaucratized schooling from a more theorized position. I was intrigued with the notion of "unschooling" as a revolutionary act, and spent a great deal of my time working on alternative education projects.

In my youthful naivete, I assumed that these critical writers, to whom I was so drawn, existed somehow "outside the system" (as though that were possible!). It never occurred to me that there might be a home for this sort of thinking in the profession of education. I had no mentors to guide me toward a profession in higher education, having been the first member of either side of my family even to attend college. Imagine my surprise when I (somewhat grudgingly) "hung up my activist's hat" to become an education professor and discovered the rich, eclectic, and radical body of literature in the field of curriculum studies! What intrigued me was the very real possibility of integrating politics and profession; all of my passions—feminism, environmental and other activist discourses, progressive politics and Marxist analysis, spirituality and the arts—were nurtured and cultivated in the various curriculum theory texts I read.

So I became a "professor" of education (although teaching as I do in a small, experimental, progressive college here in Vermont, I do very little "professing" and a lot of listening, facilitating, and dialoguing). I confess to an ongoing, committed love affair with theory, which seems to only grow with the years. Despite this perhaps suspicious tendency, I remain an activist at heart. I have come to appreciate the power of an activism informed by ongoing theoretical engagement, as well as the power of a theory that grows organically out of daily practice.

Although the 30 or so years during which I have been involved in education have seen relatively little change in what goes on in classrooms (at least in terms of the radical rethinking of the aims and purposes of education that I once hoped for), I am still idealistic about the possibilities that exist for making schools more humane, more just, more democratic, and more exciting places to be. It was this sense of hope and optimistic idealism that drew me into taking an active role these past few years in the development of Vermont state policy around a new curriculum framework. As noted in Chapter 2, I was impressed with the grass-roots, democratic origins of the statewide conversation about "what every child should know and be able to do in the 21st century," and I was curious about how far a curriculum theorist might be able to "push the envelope" in terms of bringing to the policy table the kind of analysis and critique central to curriculum studies. What I discovered, perhaps predictably, was that curriculum theory, while certainly not excluded from the conversation, played a rather secondary role to the political pull and tug of ideas around instructional methodology, content and disciplinary ideas, and assessment practices: the "techne" of daily practice. While I met and worked with scores of thoughtful and intelligent people, who were conversant with the various literatures on learning theory, cognition, and instructional methodologies, I met few who had encountered the more critical cultural analysis found in the curriculum studies literature. I felt that the conversations were limited to ideas about "what works" and the discourse of "best practices," with inadequate attention to the more substantive questions: What kind of world do we want to live in? How can schools become more democratic? How could schools be places where children and young adults really want to be? Or, to paraphrase George Counts (1932), "dare the schools even think about the possibilities for a new social order?" This is not to say that there were not innumerable progressive-minded people working on the development of Vermont's *Framework*. I sincerely believe that their commitment to creating educational environments that might foster equity, inquiry, creativity, and, to some extent, critical thinking, shows up at least implicitly in the document that we collectively created. I also believe, however, that the potential dynamism of the curriculum deliberation process has been constrained and that we have reached what Noel Gough insightfully calls "homeostasis" (see Chapter 4), largely because the discourses of accountability, standards, and best practices came to overshadow the discourses of justice, equity, caring, and human development.

The members of our Vermont study group saw themselves as progressive educators committed to these latter democratic ideals. At the same time, they had a profound awareness of the political nature of their work. Unlike theorists, whose theorizing is mostly unconstrained by political fetters, these workers must take into account the public pulse and "package" their ideas in language that is determined not to offend the sensibilities of interest groups on either end of the political spectrum. In these circumstances, it is challenging to remain faithful to cherished ideals and not "shape-shift" according to the exigencies of the political moment. This effort to maintain their integrity, often in the face of opposition or hostility, characterized the work of these curriculum leaders, but there is no denying the underlying fears and tensions that these educators, consciously or unconsciously, live with on a daily basis. As practitioners, they often found themselves in the position of negotiating between what they and other teachers really felt was in the best interests of students, and what the prevailing public education discourses demanded. This was nowhere more clear than in relation to the current prevailing discourse on standards. Theorists have taken on the notion of standards from a critical perspective, noting the ways in which they are in fact behavioral objectives wearing new clothes; the ways in which they have been neutralized of their potential moral force; the ways in which they deskill teachers by limiting their autonomy in the classroom; the ways in which they represent the demands of the corporate world for a more highly skilled, self-managed worker; and the ways in which they still work to sift and sort students along predictable lines of race, class, and gender (see Miller, 1995). Curriculum theorists will not lose their jobs by critiquing the system. In fact, as academics, this is a noble and acceptable role, and often leads to tenure. The price of this freedom is, of course, irrelevance. Practitioners, on the other hand, must mediate between the conflicting imperatives of liberatory curriculum discourses and a public and a profession that does not necessarily share the same critical consciousness about the economic and cultural forces that limit human freedom. They therefore must work more "subversively," seeking out the interstices—those spaces in between things—in which democratic curricular ideals might flourish. They are more likely to manipulate the standards to liberatory advantage, helping their colleagues extract the democratic and empowering essence of these new aims and purposes of schooling, than they are to confront and critique them directly. Our conversations always reflected this essential theory/practice tension, which is related to the relative degrees of academic freedom enjoyed by education professors and public school educators.

What do curriculum leaders need from curriculum theorists in order to create the kind of robust theory/practice dialectic that we have been seeking through the course of writing this book? While one of the group members, Kerrin McCadden, will address this question most eloquently in the closing pages of this chapter, I want to offer just a few reflections based on my ongoing conversations with the group. The issue of language and the accessibility of ideas came up often in our conversations. This is a complaint that theorists are all too familiar with, and an issue that remains unresolved in the field of curriculum studies. The question is really about whether complex historical, psychoanalytical, aesthetic, sociological, and philosophical ideas, which constitute the underpinnings of curriculum theory, can be expressed in everyday language. The answer, I believe, is yes and no. I am, on the one hand, committed to the notion that ideas should be communicated in language that reaches the intended audience. Who do curriculum theorists want to speak to? What actualities do they want to affect? If it is teachers and administrators who work 10- and 12-hour days, seeing hundreds of students and shuffling scores of papers, and schools that exist in complicated political networks, then ideas will have to be accessible. On the other hand, language theorists now talk about the ways in which language really shapes our reality and constructs what is possible. If this is so, then theorists need to continue to be playful with language, use it to stretch the "common boundaries," and open up new possibilities for practice. In this sense, theory clearly needs to remain unconstrained by discourses that would limit it to the pragmatic.

Theorists tend to eschew the concrete in the presentation of their ideas. One practitioner, for example, spoke about how much she enjoyed the writing of theorists such as David Purpel and Henry Giroux, but noted how frustrated she was that they didn't put forth any concrete prescriptions for practice. The reasoning behind this is very clear: Theorists want to facilitate more complex and liberatory ways of thinking so that practitioners will see more options for their practice, but they don't want to impose specifics, in the interest of human freedom and creativity. Critical theorists are critical of top-down mandates, even ones that might come from within their own ranks! Liberatory theorists are also sensitive to the ways in which models and examples tend to reify, and thus limit the possibilities of, their ideas. If, however, we are going to foster a rich theory/practice discussion, then theorists may have to muddle about in the concrete.

To play with the metaphor of the concrete for a moment, the word does indeed signify hard and impermeable surfaces upon which one can walk, run, and even drive heavy machinery. Concrete is, indeed, rigid and almost immovable when dry, except with a great application of force. But there is a moment of artistry in the life of concrete, in which it is pliable, fluid, and amenable to infinite shapings, limited only by the forms and frameworks that have been built to hold it. Perhaps these are the moments for the most fruitful conversations between theorists and practitioners, the moments of artistry when forms and frameworks are being built, and when the construction materials are still in a fluid state. In these moments, theorists and practitioners might become allies in the opening up of transformative possibilities. The limit of this metaphor of the "concrete," of course, is that curriculum, even in its "concrete" implementation phase, should never become rigid and inflexible, but should (ideally) remain fluid and responsive to changing conditions and student interests.

Finally, these curriculum leaders asked on a number of occasions, What are the connecting threads between the various curriculum discourses? What are the shared assumptions, the values even, that constitute a coherent body of work? Is such coherence desirable or even possible? The opening chapters of this book noted the clash and cohesion of the field as it has struggled to redefine itself against the backdrop of an earlier field devoted to ideas of scientific management, social engineering, and controlled curriculum design and development. In many ways, the curriculum field is now described best as an intertextual conversation— a dance of discourses—in which ambiguity is celebrated, paradox reigns, and uncertainty prevails. Can you imagine, politically speaking, trying to sell this to a general public crying for certainty and accountability as a description of its schools?

Curriculum theorists are not willing to give up our poststructural commitments or our emancipatory concerns. Schools as sites of contested ideals and beliefs are not likely to become less politicized in the near future. What, then, can we do to lessen this theory/practice chasm? I would like to think that we could make the lively field of curriculum studies available to an ever-expanding audience of readers and writers. Beyond this, I believe that we must engage in moral conversations and in acts of political solidarity with our colleagues in the field who struggle daily to actualize emancipatory ideals. This book has been an effort to find those liberatory points of departure from which such moral conversations and acts of solidarity might begin.

KERRIN'S REFLECTIONS

I am surprised at my terror in writing the last pages of this book. It is surprising in that I am an English teacher, who ought to relish the chance to write for a book. Terror comes, ironically, even though I am an English teacher, because I am writing something that someone else actually will read. I became a teacher, as most do, because I love my field. I had fantasies of becoming a teacher so I could be surrounded by people who practice the arts of literary existence, and students who might have the potential to care about being literary. I thought I could continue my life as a poet.

Anyone who has been where I am now is free to laugh at this point. I rarely write, except college recommendations, and poems that I manage to write during class alongside my students. These poems are all the same length, skeletons born of 10-minute poetry exercises. I do not read except to read the same books year after year, content at least that I have been able to choose some of them—and pleased to have a dozen readings of *Hamlet* under my belt, four of *Crime and Punishment*. Brilliant colleagues who are pathologically busy surround me. Gone are the small coffee-houses and the intimate circle of friends who write, read, and mull over each other's ideas.

I teach English in a small city in rural New England. I am an 80% teacher, teaching four classes: two more or less heterogeneously grouped sophomore English courses; advanced placement English, a college-level, homogeneous class; and genealogy, a multiage, heterogeneous, interdisciplinary study of family, culture, and literature. I have always had naggingly strong ideas about education and what it should and should not be—a generative, honest exchange of thoughts and feelings, rather than simple banking and recycling of stale concepts. Moving minute to minute from class to class, there is little time to communicate with others about these ideas that struggle to catch up with me throughout the day. I thought if I were to take on the new role of Humanities Department curriculum coordinator, I would get to dwell more in a world of ideas.

The Humanities Department is an umbrella for English, foreign languages, social studies, fine arts, and the library. This turned out to be more of a paper shuffling, meeting over lunch, budgetary experience than an opportunity for true, collegial connection and philosophical play. Part of this job is a weekly lunch hour gathering of the curriculum team, made up of a group of teacher leaders from diverse areas. For 2 months there has been a dangling agenda item that never makes it to the top of our list: "challenging curriculum." We take care of school-wide minutiae. We perform tasks and organize things. I do not mean this to sound tongue in cheek. These things must be taken care of, but what of nurturing the coherent vision? With more of a vacuum where I had hoped to find thoughts, I decided to write a grant to make time to study a particularly nagging idea: gender fairness and the humanities curriculum. I then became Project Director for a school-to-work project called "The Whole Story." Then, I agreed to work on this book.

After looking back on this paragraph and remembering that I have a family, friends, a dog, a farm, and some shred of a life, I think I must have been losing my mind to embroil myself in so many disparate (albeit thematically connected) pursuits. In fact, I've found that that's precisely why I did each thing: I was losing my mind. I don't mean this in the idiomatic sense. I was not going crazy, although craziness was certainly part of the net effect. I was losing, and mourning, my living mind. I began writing an as yet nameless book about curriculum reform regarding gender. It seemed logical to begin with a brief introduction describing the dominant culture's attitudes throughout the ages toward women's minds; this was to yield a few summary pages of background.

I sought to put into perspective a humanities curriculum that still largely enjoys the freedom to ignore the collective experiences of women. After 20 pages of writing, I was still nowhere near the present day and found myself deeply obsessed with writing a survey of 3 thousand years of the same idea about women: keep them busy so they will not think. This was not surprising—this last idea. I had known what I would find. I was so busy that I did not recognize that my quest to uncover the cultural context for women's minds mirrored my own quest. In scurrying, over-loading-my-plate activity, I was hunting—although I lacked clear method—for a life of the mind.

Women's minds have been alternately feared and dismissed, at least since Aristotle. The enticing vision of a bustled, bustling woman with busy hands and an idle mind is one of the hallmarks of Victorian society. In preparation for a life of companionship with her husband (her crown-ing glory), a woman busied herself not in studying the latest philosophers, reading the next Russian novel on her reading list, working out the glitches in her latest calculus problem or mechanical invention, or reading the latest science journals, but, as far into the wee hours as available light-ing would permit, in hand-tatting lace and stitching and embroidering delicate garments for her trousseau.

Like any self-respecting Victorian era woman, classroom teachers have been given too much lace to tat and too many knick-knacks to dust to nurture ideas. This book is about *praxis*—the link between theory and what people can, should, will do with it. As it stands, educational theorists are not primary or secondary school teachers; they are largely professors who inhabit worlds that both enable and expect them to have a life of the mind.

Theory is an art, and a playful one in its highest form, but, at the very least, theory is built on creative vision. Artists perform simple tasks, dipping brush into water, making brushstrokes, but before they perform these productive tasks, their minds must play. They need time to make vision. The world is churned about in the brain, collected into some co-herent whole, and expressed. The expression cannot come without the playfulness of the churning, and the churning cannot happen without space and time and a certain kind of comfort, whether it is provided by a patron or a refusal to do dishes.

Theory tends toward language that plays, tempts, seduces, and un-veils—curvy logic and doubling back mark its best moments, and give evidence of a creative mind at play. As long as teachers run their days on a factory-style gerbil wheel, except for that short, sweet blast of theory we get as we begin our teaching careers in graduate school, theory becomes a knick-knack in the life of the practicing teacher.

At our high school, thoughts and theories are largely eclipsed by a mind-numbing number of meetings and acronyms. Each teacher is re-quired to take part in an Educational Support Team (EST), the purpose of which is a combination of helping case manage troubled students and helping support faculty members. In reality, only a small percentage of the time in many ESTs is spent helping teachers. There are Individualized

Educational Plans (IEPS) for Special Ed. students. Each teacher has 10–15 students on IEPS and thus is required to attend a lengthy planning meeting for each student, most often clumped at the start of the academic year. There are Personal Learning Plans (PLPS) that teachers must manage within the Teacher Advisory (TA) group. In each TA group is an average of four freshman students. For each of these this year, and for all freshmen and sophomores next year, and so on, the TA group must have three parent/TA/student conferences (often outside of school time), to help navigate each student's education toward a path that holds meaning and fosters passion. PLPS are new this year, and the program was brilliantly designed to give teachers even more to do. Prior Mutual Expectations (PMES) is a goals document that each teacher leader needs to work from; it is a list of what we expect from ourselves. There are weekly inservice trainings during which we often trudge through the interminable work of aligning our school with the state's standards document, often in a way that is not consistent with its spirit. If we are not using our weekly inservice time to work on standards, we are working on PLP training.

Time rarely is sanctioned for working on other curricular issues, and departments must work on these during meetings outside of the school day. Each teacher is required to work on an Organizational Team (School Climate, Diversity, Technology). There is the Monday afternoon nuts and bolts meeting where we do the fine tuning and necessary venting. Our school is a Professional Development School (PDS), a "teaching hospital" for university students studying education. Every year, we have 10 or so teacher interns who work side by side with faculty members to learn how to teach. Tremendous teacher energy goes into this program. There is a powerful and wonderful Strategic Plan in the implementation phase, which needs constant attention and care. Beyond all this, there are also duties: cafeteria, quiet study, planning room, detention duty after school. There are after-school departmental meetings for the Humanities Department, the Science, Math, and Technology Department, and the smaller, traditional departments. Next week, budgets are due. All of the innovative elements, to their credit, exist to support teaching, and the faculty is a risk-taking, willing, professional, intellectually exciting faculty. Each initiative (there are more) has all the best intentions and has helped rank our school among the top five PDS institutions in the nation. Teaching students, you will notice, is not included anywhere in this vast list.

This intense scurrying is most effective at keeping us from truly thinking. Perhaps our problem is that we are so willing to do all these things. I can't remember the last time I had a week that allowed me the time—without forsaking something else—to design a new "unit." Because I've always promised myself I would retire if I ever had a "November Folder," I fear this stasis. My teaching cannot change, nor can I build or find the ideas necessary to its nurture, if I am required to do this much hustling. I want my ideas to be respected so much that they are required of me. It needs to be my job to be alive and growing.

As Garrison (1997) writes: "Monism is dogmatism" (p. 15). We are fractured in our daily lives as teachers; we do one thing over all others, we scurry. This is the dogmatic scourge. We are told what to do by the monotony of our chores, and thus we struggle to grow. As discussed in Chapter 1, "the strong democrat engages in a continuous, lifelong dialogical inquiry that deepens her/his understanding of the interdependence of all living things." These are words beautiful enough to make any kind of democracy sound good, but, to be a strong democrat, this is the dream of the thoughtful teacher, not easily the reality. Moments of true inquiry happen in teachers' lives only when stolen.

Currently, we think as we talk, perched on table edges in impromptu dialogues. We form ideas as we gather around the brain of the school, the copy machine. We may even make more and more work for ourselves so that we can see one another and perform the dialectical dances we need to keep growing. We are certainly not dead, but we are suffering. One teacher recently told me that if I ever left him, it would be the end of him. We are not having an affair, but we do share ideas.

In watching this book take shape, I stole away again and again from "work" in order to share ideas and I encountered minds filled with beautiful thoughts about teaching and learning. Gail McCutcheon explores deliberation as it applies to the lives of teachers. In an institution rife with conflict to an often tiresome degree, it is good to be reminded that "conflict is to be cherished." If we tire too quickly of the conflicts that surround ideas, we rush toward solutions, losing the "full examination of the alternatives," and possibly losing the ability to reach the best solutions. It is also good to be reminded that the hurried, on-the-spot planning that often happens in the classroom while we scrap plans and move with the current of student needs is a good thing, that it marks an ability to deliberate for the sake of learning—that it is not a sign of overwhelming inadequacies.

It is not only teachers who struggle to maintain a lively mind. Sloughing off layers of the modernist tradition of education, we begin to find the core that is true education. It is similar to the core we find if we begin to slough off a student's layers of dead knowledge. As we might find honest and earnest learning when we take away the metaphoric walls of school, at the core of each student we might find selves rich enough to be the basis for curriculum. We are often afraid to include the depths and spirit of the student as we design or implement what we teach. While school itself seems to work against truly knowing any of the humans within it on a spiritual level, there are strategies to help bring a mythopoetic focus to curriculum: journals; asking for subjective reader response rather than objective answers to factual questions; using student-generated autobiographies as text; theater and role playing; student-generated poetry, art and dance as means of responding to most kinds of learning; writing prose snapshots of remembered ideas; and storytelling. Where schooling often offers precious few avenues toward knowledge, for Kesson the arts in a mythopoetic curriculum "provide a pluralistic approach to cognition and offer multiple entry points into concepts and ideas, [provoking] students into newer, more complex understandings." If we place the student at the center of the curriculum, the student is enabled to participate fully in building ideas.

Virginia Woolf knew that to indulge in ideas, one needed certain supports, a room of one's own, and money enough to buy leisure. It is a stark reality that few people have the luxury that once was afforded the thinking men of history: a household that was structured to ease his every movement—silence, food, sleep when he needed each. Over the past months, a group of us read, studied, and discussed the chapters of this book. In the great balancing act, I know reading essays on theory to be less important than playing Legos and reading books with my daughter. Reading these essays began when my daughter finally would submit to sleep and all other nightly rituals were accomplished, after 11 o'clock.

Nearing midnight, Noel Gough's chapter was no picnic, but it was rapture of a sort to dig through it. I wrote passages of this chapter in my car, leaning against the steering wheel, at one o'clock in the morning, after losing an argument with myself that I could memorize the words until morning; while teaching class; and by kicking my family out of the house during family time. My school did grant me 2 days professional leave to write. This bodes well for us: Time for thinking—and even "thinking requirements"—are on the horizon for public school teachers. Perhaps then the media, given ample evidence finally that we do think, will stop indulging the public in teacher bashing. It is, after all, terribly unbecoming. Best of all, perhaps some of us will write a book like this. Perhaps it is not more access to theory that teachers need, but rather room for theory making, lively minds, paintbrushes, and visions.

I like to pretend I am a fledgling performance artist, which brings this back to artistry again. It is always good to think we are artists—to consciously try to dissociate from the factory. What if I wanted to write a book, and count myself also an educational theorist? What would I need? I would need all of the things circling about in the preceding paragraphs: room, time, space, and support. Instead of making sure I was busy counting heads, generating scores, attending meetings, aligning myself with standards, following protocol, I would make sure I was thinking, inquiring, growing. I would make time in my workday when I must study. Let me have meaningful homework. I wouldn't relegate my studies to the courses I must take to keep my teaching license; I would create them to deal directly with my life and the lifetimes my students spend with me. I would teach one fewer class and would myself take a course called Scholarship. I would study anything from "The Philosophy of Administering Quizzes and Their Effects on Community-Building Efforts" to "Rebellious Poetry" or "The Church in the Russian Novel"—anything that would take me on an intellectual journey. If each teacher had time sanctioned (or even mandated) for study, the school would be on fire. I know that without witnessing teacher scholarship, my students learn some uncalculated lessons. If I can find no other time to initiate my own poetic inspiration than during class, how can I say that writing poetry is like breathing, that writing is a way of living? If I can only scribble short notes on the ends of papers, what thoughtful revision can I inspire? If I forget what it means to make ideas, what loss to us all if they follow suit?

Years ago, a writer wrote a novel about unrequited love on the moors, a novella about an office clerk turned dung-beetle, a novella about a woman creeping around a yellow room on all fours, biting furniture. Each delighted in some way in representing her or his world. Years later came the "afterings," the essays that mark the signposts in each—what each says to us about who we are. Theory both makes sense of what is and confounds what we perceive. Literary theory endlessly loops around human experience, searching. It is the play of otters, delighting in ideas for their own sake. In the postmodern, deconstructionist age, literary theory reminds me that literature is more profound than the most profound thought. The mere fact that countless readings can emerge from the same piece of literature, is the signifier that literature—which is, in the end, concentrated human experience—holds more than we can know. It is this mythic dimension that also emerges in classrooms and in ideas about learning. We are bound by an ethic of care to play hard with ideas about education. As with literature, every time we write about education, it expands, grows both more real and more mythic.

The art of writing about education is not, however, the same as the art of teaching. As teachers turn toward theory, given that we especially bear the shadow of factory workers gone by (we are ourselves experiments in time-and-motion), we always want to know the practical applications of theories. What are the steps to Kincheloe's chapter, "Critical Democracy and Education"? Critical pedagogy refuses us the traditional instruction manual; otherwise it could make no claims to postmodernity, or to liberatory pedagogy, and would be yet another modernist iteration of the same old, same old. In crashing down the factory tradition that is so much still the foundation of the schooling life, critical theorists seek instead to incite an ever-changing curriculum—to engage learners, both students and teachers, in inquiry that uncovers all built assumptions. They thankfully would have us eschew the sacred neutrality of the public school and expose ourselves as human after all. By pretending neutrality, we teach that hierarchy, not community, forms knowledge; students learn that learning means isolated minds on a sterile plane.

What might critical theory do to inform teaching on a day-by-day basis? It might make us rethink, once and for all, homogeneously grouped classrooms where the socially and economically well-off rise to the top not because of their inherently better raw intellectual material, but because, for example, they don't need 25-hour-a-week, after-school jobs. I think also of the power and trust handed over to a class when they choose a novel to read and as a community—which includes the teacher as both learner and knower—undertake a study, themselves searching for the questions and generating the meanings. Teaching young people to uncover the workings of power and how power shapes consciousness, graces people with images of what is possible. If we deconstruct, for example, the canon of questions about literature that continually is "bought and sold" by teachers and fed to students, we can ask students instead to write the questions—the set of concerns and curiosity we have for the fictitious world. In doing so, students are freed from a leash-led "inquiry" of the world. In the grasp of a liberated intellect, literature has more potential as a lens through which to examine lives and ages. Carrying "emancipation" a step further, think dangerously of teachers "teaching" books that they have never read and do not read even as the class is reading them; in this way, teachers might free students completely from the idea that students need traditional teacher input in order to develop a valid interpretation of a novel—it also would be great fun in its undeniable defiance of the modernist pedagogical model.

And as we refuse to follow traditional, handed-down directions about how to ensure production rather than creation in our classrooms, so we can perform similar stunts with handed-down directives from the administrative sphere. In Gough's chapter, we are warned against turning "documents into monuments." As one well acquainted with the onslaught of *Frameworks* and *Standards,* I am also well acquainted with the trend to deify such documents. It is easy to be moved to homeostasis by something called a standards framework; it is easy to allow it to cease to be a document of possibility and become reified as a material object, especially given the strata of "control" and "organization" above which we struggle to rise. The idea of deconstructing this "text" in much the same way literature can be deconstructed is exhilarating: "to destabilize texts— to make them yield unexpected conclusions." I'm not yet sure how to destabilize a framework or how to transfer the skills for deconstructing literature to deconstructing a framework, but if it takes flying across a few continents for tea with Noel Gough, I'll do it.

A framework can, I think, be liberatory; but not if it invites us to sit still for too long. There is a false conception that all is right in the world as long as what we teach fits the framework—that if we teach "standards-based units," we are great teachers. If we get complacent, reflexivity ends. "The ghost in the curriculum" emerges, and we cease ourselves to be emergent. Gough asks, "How can we act to reflexively disturb the equilibrium of the systems in which we work, to provide opportunities for unpredictable, complex, and unstable outputs to emerge?" We can refuse to teach to curriculum documents. When asked to "align" one of our units to the document to make sure we are marching in step, first we can say, perhaps, that we have no units, that we teach from day to day according to what happens in the classroom communities for which we are stewards; second, we can ask questions about the value of aligning what we do to an external document—where will this bring us? If I understand Gough, it is not necessarily that we must pester both the document and the administration, but that we must question continually what the existence of this document means—what, by its existence, does it leave out? What value system does it propagate? What could we do without it that we can't do with it? What is the "noise" that is behind this document?

The assumption that I have organized my teaching moments into quantifiable, concrete entities that might, assuming they can be called to order, be sorted into compartments is a very loud "noise" in my world. Running down a rattling conveyor belt, my ideas for teaching *The Color Purple* (Walker, 1982) are invoiced and listed on a packing slip as if they were stable things pulled from a shelf. How am I to resist homeostasis when my teaching is to be boxed? With recursive looping and reflexivity we reject stasis. Telling "stories that never end" involves reading and subsequently rejecting part or all of that reading, never seeing the document the same way twice. We learn to "read" the document so it becomes generative.

This word, "generative," threads its way through almost every idea in this book. Even when we are being reminded to deconstruct, it is for the sake of continued change and growth. When we are asked to embrace conflict, conflict gives birth. When we are brave enough to struggle for a mythopoetic curriculum, students and teachers can uncover untold awareness. It is vital to condition ourselves as educators to feel a cold shiver every time we begin to think we know any of the answers. This kind of comfort never inspired vision.

REFERENCES

Cherryholmes, C. H. (1988). *Power and criticism: Poststructural investigations in education.* New York: Teachers College Press.

Counts, G. S. (1932). *Dare the school build a new social order?* New York: John Day.

Dewey, J. (1963). *Experience and education.* New York: Collier Books. (Original work published 1938)

Eisner, E. W. (1994). *Cognition and curriculum reconsidered* (2nd ed.). New York: Teachers College Press.

Garrison, J. (1997). *Dewey and eros: Wisdom and desire in the art of teaching.* New York: Teachers College Press.

Giroux, H. A. (1992). *Bordercrossings.* New York: Routledge.

Jackson, P. W. (1992). Conceptions of curriculum and curriculum specialists. In P. W. Jackson (Ed.), *Handbook of research on curriculum* (pp. 3–40). New York: Macmillan.

LePage, A. (1987). *Transforming education: The new 3R's.* Oakland: Oakmore House.

Marsh, C., & Willis, G. (1995). *Curriculum: Alternative approaches, ongoing issues.* Englewood Cliffs, NJ: Merrill.

Miller, R. (Ed.). (1995). *Educational freedom for democratic society.* Brandon, VT: Holistic Education Press.

Moore, T. (1996). *The re-enchantment of everyday life.* New York: HarperCollins.

Pinar, W. F., Reynolds, W. M., Slattery, P., & Taubman, P. M. (1995). *Understanding curriculum: An introduction to the study of historical and contemporary curriculum discourses.* New York: Peter Lang.

Portelli, J. P. (1987). Perspectives and imperatives on defining curriculum. *Journal of Curriculum and Supervision, 2*(4), 354–367.

Walker, A. (1982). *The color purple.* New York: Simon & Schuster Pocket Books.

Whitman, W. (1992). *Leaves of grass.* New York: Simon & Schuster/Quality Paperback Book Club. (Original work published 1855)

About the Editors and the Contributors

Noel Gough is Associate Professor and Deputy Director, Deakin Centre for Education and Change, Deakin University, Victoria, Australia. His research interests include narrative theory and popular media culture in education, with particular reference to qualitative research methodologies, curriculum change, environmental education, and science education. He is the Australian Editor of the *Journal of Curriculum Studies* and an Executive Editor of *The Australian Educational Researcher,* and has published extensively in his areas of research interest.

James G. Henderson (Editor) is Professor of Curriculum and Instruction at Kent State University and has served as chair of the Critical Issues in Curriculum Special Interest Group of the American Educational Research Association. His research has focused on curriculum and teaching practices informed by multitextual curriculum studies and democratic progressive ideals. He is author of two texts on caring and collegial teaching practices*: Reflective Teaching: Becoming an Inquiring Educator* and *Reflective Teaching: The Study of Your Constructivist Practices.* He also has co-authored a book on democratic curriculum practices entitled *Transformative Curriculum Leadership,* the second edition of which is currently in press. He recently served as guest editor for two issues of the journal *Teaching Education,* on the topic of transformative curriculum leadership.

Kathleen R. Kesson (Editor) is Director of Teacher Education at Goddard College, an experimental college in central Vermont founded on the principles of John Dewey. She is also Research Associate Professor at the University of Vermont, where she directs the John Dewey Project on Progressive Education. She has published a number of papers that explore critical and philosophical dimensions of spirituality and holistic education.

Joe L. Kincheloe is a Professor of Cultural Studies and Pedagogy at Penn State University. He has published several books in curriculum, foundations, critical pedagogy, and cultural studies. His latest books include *Students as Researchers* (with Shirley Steinberg) and *How Do We Tell the Workers? The Socio-Economic Foundations of Work and Vocational Education.*

Kerrin A. McCadden is a high school English teacher at Montpelier High School in Montpelier, Vermont. She is currently Chair of the Humanities Department at her school and is involved in a study of gender bias in the curriculum.

Gail McCutcheon's research has centered on teacher thinking and curriculum development. She teaches courses in curriculum studies at Ohio State University.

Index